THE LANGUAGE OF DRAMA
Critical Theory and Practice

David Birch

MACMILLAN

First published 1991 by
THE MACMILLAN PRESS LTD
Houndmills, Basingstoke, Hampshire RG21 2XS
and London
Companies and representatives
throughout the world

ISBN 0–333–51637–0 hardcover
ISBN 0–333–51638–9 paperback

A catalogue record for this book is available
from the British Library

Printed in Hong Kong

Reprinted 1992

Contents

If you just let a play
speak, it may not make
a sound.
>   (Peter Brook)

For
Frederick Birch
1923–90

Then I saw that the wall had never been there,
that the 'unheard-of' is here and this, not
something and somewhere else.

(Dag Hammarskjöld)

Acknowledgements

This book was completed during an overseas study programme granted to me by Murdoch University, Western Australia, which I took up as a Visiting Fellow in the Department of English Studies, University of Nottingham, UK. I would like to thank Ron Carter, in particular, for the support he gave to me during this fellowship; the staff of the Hallward Library, Cripps Computing Centre and Cripps Hall; the careful and detailed attention Norman Blake, the general editor of this series, gave to this book in preparation; and the highly skilled secretarial support given to me by remote control from Jan Bide in Perth.

My debt to contemporary theorists and drama scholarship is a large one. If I have failed to give due notice of particular contributions directly in the text, recognition of the contribution is acknowledged in the References and Bibliography. Furthermore my colleagues in the School of Humanities, Murdoch University, are a continual source of stimulation. I should record my debt in particular to those colleagues and students who were engaged in the debates (and battles) about semiotics, theatre and drama praxis; to Tan See Kam, whose comments were invaluable, and to David George, David Moody, Serge Tampalini, Jenny de Reuck, Anthea Gupta and John Frow for critical comment on earlier drafts.

The author and publishers wish to thank the following who have kindly given permission for the use of copyright material:

Alan Bold for material from *The State of the Nation*, Chatto and Windus, 1969; Jonathan Cape Ltd. for material from *Who's Afraid of Virginia Woolf*; and with the Estate of Eugene O'Neill for material from *The Iceman Cometh*; Rosica Colin Ltd. on behalf of the author for material from *Greek* by Steven Berkoff. Copyright ©

Steven Berkoff 1980, 1982, 1983, 1986, 1989; and *East* by Steven
Berkoff. Copyright © Steven Berkoff 1977, 1978; Grafton Books
for material from *Boys from the Blackstuff* by Alan Bleasdale;
Grove Press for material from *American Buffalo* by David Mamet,
1977; A. M. Heath and Co. Ltd. on behalf of the author for
material from *Home* by David Storey, Jonathan Cape; Heinemann
Publishers (Oxford) Ltd. for material from *Six Characters in
Search of an Author* by L. Pirandello; Methuen London for
material from *Being and Nothingness* by Jean-Paul Sartre, 1957,
The Worlds by Edward Bond, 1980; *Softcops*, 1983, *Traps*, 1978,
and *Cloud Nine*, 1979 by Caryl Churchill; *The Complete Fawlty
Towers* by John Cleese and Connie Booth, 1988; *Elizabeth:
Almost by Chance* by Dario Fo, 1987; *The Ride Across Lake
Constance*, 1973 and *Kaspar*, 1969, by Peter Handke; *The Ruffian
on the Stair* by Joe Orton, 1967; *Betrayal*, 1978, *Old Times*, 1971,
The Dwarfs, 1977, and *The Caretaker*, 1960, by Harold Pinter;
Shout Across the River, 1979, and *Caught on a Train*, 1982, by
Stephen Poliakoff; *The Pope's Wedding* by Edward Bond, 1977;
Poppy by Peter Nichols, 1982; *Painting a Wall* by David Lan,
1979; *Comedians* by Trevor Griffiths, 1976; and *Fish in the Sea* by
John McGrath, 1977; Oxford University Press for material from
Boesman and Lena, 1980, and *Sizwe Bansi is Dead*, 1974, by Athol
Fugard; and 'The Road' in *Collected Plays*, 1973, and *A Dance of
the Forests*, 1963, by Wole Soyinka; Margaret Ramsey Ltd. on
behalf of the author for material from *Season's Greetings* by Alan
Ayckbourn. Copyright © Haydonning Ltd.; Tanner Propp Fersko
and Sterner on behalf of the author for material from *Four
Dynamic Plays* by Ed Bullins.

Every effort has been made to trace all the copyright holders
but if any have been inadvertently overlooked the publishers
will be pleased to make the necessary arrangement at the first
opportunity.

Foreword

The Language of Drama may sit somewhat polemically in a series called *The Language of Literature*, if by 'literature' readers expect a critical practice theoretically based on the canons and orthodoxies of Anglo-American new criticism. If, however, 'literature' is seen in terms of a wider, more discursive, context, which is theoretically based in contemporary social semiotics and critical practice, then *The Language of Drama* will sit rather more comfortably in such a series.

'Comfortable' is a relative term. There are ideas and views in this book which will challenge both received and radical drama criticism amongst those who use drama for classroom purposes, and those who use drama for production purposes. I draw together both of those concerns, and others, in a framework of contemporary language, literature, discourse, culture and semiotics theories, to develop a social, critical practice for the analysis of the language(s) of drama texts.

The Language of Drama, therefore, is different to the rather more traditional literary approaches to the language of drama texts (for example, Brown, 1972; Kennedy, 1975; Evans, 1977) and to the more formal semiotic approaches (for example, Elam, 1980; Pfister, 1988) in a number of important ways.

First of all, my approach to language is developed out of an interdisciplinary concern for bringing together many of the insights into language made in contemporary critical, linguistic, cultural, philosophical, sociological and political theories. This results in a critical practice which is as concerned with social meaning and cultural practices of discourse as it is with detailed linguistic analysis of words and sentences. In that sense, then, what is involved is a practice of language analysis which is concerned both with the detailed description of language structures

1

and with the broadening of what constitutes those structures socially, politically and discursively, as part of a *social semiotic*.

Second, my approach involves a redefining of the drama text, away from the narrow concept of it as a literary 'play' which is 'brought to life' on stage, or which can be discussed in the same critical terms as a poem or novel, to an understanding of how it means, socially, politically and discursively, according to the various uses made of it in widely differing performance contexts.

The critical vocabulary for doing this is quite different to that used in the more traditional literary and linguistic approaches to texts. I hope that *The Language of Drama* will function as a means of introducing many of the important ideas and practices of contemporary critical theory and language analysis to students of drama; particularly as drama has, in comparison to other discourses and genres, attracted so little attention from language theorists and analysts.

My approach is also a politically committed one. I am concerned with developing a theory of *drama praxis* which argues for a social theory of language based on conflict rather than the more usual co-operation, and for a social theory of drama based on the political and institutional uses to which texts can be put. Taken together, this involves a theory of drama praxis which calls for action in the form of change, both in terms of classroom and production practices involving drama, and in the larger institutional (ideological) practices of society.

I am not an innocent, disinterested, academic observer of texts, but, as I developed in some detail in *Language, Literature and Critical Practice* (Birch, 1989a), I am concerned with a critical theory and practice which will deconstruct texts in order to demonstrate the often oppressive social/institutional practices which determine how those texts mean. This therefore involves a drama praxis which is principally concerned with the relationship of language and ideology; language and power; language and control; with issues of authorship and control of meaning; with gender; institutional oppression; multiplicity of meanings; with the way we are constructed as subjects; with open rather than closed interpretation; with choices and multiple voices; with stereotypes and performance roles; with discourse frames and conventions; with the social determination of multiple realities and fictions; with dialogue and interaction; with disturbance and defamiliarisation and with cultural power. These, and other related concerns, form the critical concerns of *The Language of Drama*, and as such are as important for those who use drama in the classroom as for those who use drama in production.

The critical theories, practices, ideas, vocabulary and texts I have chosen to exemplify points in this book have been chosen to demonstrate an interdisciplinary concern for how drama texts mean. I include a wide range of texts which are used for theatre, television, radio, film, print production and classroom analysis. I concentrate, in the main, on contemporary texts which are easily available for further study. Those texts include plays written for theatre, radio and television; filmscripts; television comedy; jokes; performance poetry; theatre reviews; academic discourse; actors writing about their work; dramatists writing about their work; directors writing about their work; publishers' blurbs and transcriptions of 'everyday' language. All of these categories of text, and more, make up the *discourse* of drama. This discourse, and my developing concern with the critical theory and practice of drama praxis, is the focus of *The Language of Drama*.

There are six chapters. The first chapter, 'Drama Praxis', discusses issues of authorship and some of the more traditional aspects of treating drama texts as literature, and establishes the need for a different, more radical, approach to understanding language and drama as part of a social semiotic. I establish what I mean by praxis; develop a communicative theory of language based on social interaction, multiple voices and multiple interpretations, and introduce the theoretically crucial notion that HOW texts mean is more important than WHAT texts mean. This involves pragmatics and performance, which in turn involves us in recognising the various ways we have of making meaning beyond the words of a text. I propose that writing, reading, analysis, rehearsal, production and reception are best considered as performance processes, and that no single interpretation of a text should ever be considered the 'right' one.

Chapter 2 'Making Sense' and Chapter 3, 'Conflict', develop some of these ideas and examine the frames and conventions of performance and production; the ways we make things sensible, and the criteria and ideologies involved in some of those ways; the realities, fictions and illusions of making sense, and the interactional control, co-operation and conflict that can result. That interaction is considered in terms of dialogism and the various goal-oriented manipulation strategies that we use in order to effect change upon someone else.

Chapter 4, 'Control', develops this further by looking at the classifications and moves that can be made in order to establish a particular role relationship, and the various language categories that can be used to support that role as a dominant/controlled one. A major part of that control is an institutional one which establishes value distinctions between standard and non-standard languages, and which prioritises standard languages and their texts and users. This creates a domination which drama praxis deconstructs and seeks to change by defamiliarisation strategies.

Chapter 5, 'Roles', continues this deconstruction by examining the various performance routines and fronts we use in inter-action, concentrating on context and appropriateness, and on the way we are constructed (interpellated) as performance subjects by the gaze of others. This involves the way we are named and the way we name others; the deixis involved in establishing person, time and place relations, and the stereotypes which can result and thereby oppress.

Chapter 6, 'Cultural Power', develops this idea of oppression by examining issues of gender, sexuality, womens' language, car-nivalesque discourse, colonial and post-colonial oppression and the praxis involved in appropriating repressive discourse and writing back in order to overthrow disabling images and ident-ities.

All six chapters, as well as the Afterword which summarises the discussion of language and praxis, are concerned with how these issues, and others, affect the discourse of drama, and what we DO with it in the various performances of reading, writing, analysis, rehearsal, production and reception. Specifically, the first two chapters form an introduction to some of the more general, theoretical, ideas of the book, and the remaining four develop these ideas more fully by a detailed analysis of the language of a wide-ranging collection of drama texts. I use these examples to demonstrate some of the specific issues affecting a critical understanding of drama discourse, and to set the agenda for developing the discussion beyond this book into the classrooms, rehearsal rooms and studios, theatres and press rooms, living rooms and studies, where those performances take place each day. Drama praxis is about social and institutional action and change. *The Language of Drama* is about effecting that action and change.

1   Drama Praxis

Authorship

When the Royal Shakespeare Company decided to produce a new play by John Arden and Margaretta D'Arcy in 1973 (*The Island of the Mighty*, later published as Arden and D'Arcy (1974), but without reference to this production), Arden and D'Arcy, who were under contract to attend rehearsals and to rewrite where necessary, reached a point where they could not understand why the actors '. . . were playing their parts so strangely' (Arden, 1977:159). When confronted, the director admitted that rehearsals had been running without the writers present because he had ideas about 'the meaning' of 'the play' which were in conflict with the writers'. Arden and D'Arcy believed that:

> . . . only the playwright can understand the meaning of a new unperformed play . . . no one else can be certain what the structure is intended to express. The business of interpretation (i.e. how the meaning is presented on stage) is the department of the director. (Arden, 1977:160)

Arden and D'Arcy considered the meaning to be quite distinct from interpretation. Meaning is an absolute reality encoded into the play by the writers. The director's job, they argued, is not to change or alter this reality but to stage it faithfully. The manner of this staging is the responsibility of the director, but the meaning isn't. The interpretation should not distort the reality of the meaning encoded into the text by the writer(s) regardless of how the staging might vary from director to director. The absolute meaning of the play will remain the same because this meaning 'belongs' not to the director but to the writer(s) and will always remain unchanged.

The director of this production clearly had different views about meaning and interpretation and went ahead against the wishes of the writers who subsequently went on strike, picketing the entrance to the theatre and withdrawing their names from the programme:

> . . . in the hope that the critics and public would realize what was on stage was alone the work of the RSC – based admittedly upon the Arden/D'Arcy script – but abridged and interpreted finally without reference to the writers and their desired meaning. (Arden, 1977:171)

This is not simply a conflict of authorship but a struggle for the control of meaning. Steven Connor writes about such a struggle in his book on Samuel Beckett and concludes that:

> If all authors fear the breaks, ruptures and discontinuities that reading, interpretation and productions bring, then to direct one's own plays is a way of extending authorial control into the act of reading or consumption, and bringing idea and embodiment, script and performance together. (Connor, 1988:186)

This may certainly extend authorial control, but does not guarantee, in any circumstances, that the meanings 'intended' by the writer are necessarily safer in the writer's hands than they are in a director's, because meanings are constantly shifting and changing – they can never be captured and made secure. As Polish director Jerzy Grotowski in *Towards a Poor Theatre* (1969:98) makes clear. 'I do not put on a play in order to teach others what I already know. It is after the production is completed and not before that I am wiser.' British dramatist Edward Bond in the introduction to *The Bundle* (1978: xviii) writes that 'The dramatist can help to create a new theatre by the way he [*sic passim*] writes. He should not dramatize the story but the analysis.' A writer's intentions are variable, because reading, analysis, production and reception of texts are variable, and recognising this allows the important concept of variable meanings to be developed – variable for both writer and reader; for director and actor; for actor and audience.

So, whilst the industrial action that Arden and D'Arcy initiated was an important political move, and one that has since been taken up by other writers, their views on meaning and interpretation reflect a traditional understanding of the role of the writer which ties intentions, desires and meanings to an individual insight which others by a process of interpretation must eventually come to share. If they do not, 'the meaning' of 'the play' 'put into the text' by the writer has not been understood and the interpretation would be considered 'faulty' (Arden, 1977:160).

This is a view developed at length within Anglo-American new criticism (for example, Heilman and Brooks, 1945) and one still held by many resulting, for example, in theatre critics still talking about '. . . the old-fashioned virtues of careful and perceptive attention to the text . . .' (David Cairns reviewing *Figaro, The Sunday Times*, 9 July 1989:C7), where the idea of 'the text' is that it is a stable, unchanging, repository of meanings which determine *the* single interpretation of the text; or of academics arguing for the drama text to be seen as a 'score' where the dialogue is '. . . the scaffolding inside which stage meanings are erected' (Styan, 1960:48).

When George Devine, for example, directed *Play* (Beckett, 1972) at the Old Vic in London in April 1964 he wrote in the programme notes:

> When working as a director on a Beckett play . . . one has to think of the text as something like a musical score wherein the 'notes', the sights, the sounds, the pauses, have their own special inter-related rhythms, and out of their composition comes the dramatic impact. (Reid, 1969:35)

Such views assert a privileged and privileging role for the literary text and its author. Alec Reid in his book on Beckett presents a typical position on this when he writes:

> The toneless voices and the rapid tempo . . . make it impossible for the actor or director to impart any personal interpretation of the roles over and above what Beckett has provided. (Reid, 1969:38)

He argues that for *Play*, there is no room for interpretation 'beyond' the play, '. . . because it's all there . . .', already. (Reid, 1969:45).

This is a view which in its general privileging of authorial 'ownership' of interpretation and meaning is increasingly challenged and rejected in contemporary critical theory. Roland Barthes, for example, in his seminal paper 'The Death of the Author' writes that 'To give a text an Author is to impose a limit on that text, to furnish it with a final signified, to close the writing' (Barthes, 1968:212), and hence, therefore, to close off interpretation. Similarly Michel Foucault in 'What is an Author' suggests that instead of asking questions like 'Who is the real author? Have we proof of his [*sic passim*] authenticity and originality?' and 'What has he revealed of his most profound self in his language?', we would be better served asking questions like 'What are the modes of existence for this discourse? Where does it come from; how is it circulated; who controls it?', and so on (Foucault, 1969:290).

Thus, while John Arden developed important ideas and practices for the politicising of the theatre and argued that '. . . the theatre of today has little or no use for the old idea of a play-text consisting of a series of speeches interspersed by a few stage-directions' (Arden, 1977:175), his view of the 'reality' of meaning is still tied to much older, more traditional empiricist liberal/humanist notions of absolutism and individualism where 'Any play of quality is expected to present a characteristic vision of the world. It is assumed that this will be the personal vision of the Dramatist . . .' (Arden, 1977:208). Dramatists should be '. . . regarded as the primary source for all the ideas (whether explicit through the spoken word or implicit in the stagecraft) which the play transmits . . .' (Arden, 1977:209). The only alternative to this, Arden writes, is the idea of the theatre collective where all participants work in partnership on all aspects of the production. But this, he conceded, rarely works successfully in practice. British theatre director Peter Brook makes a similar point when he writes that 'There is eventually a need for authorship to reach the ultimate compactness and focus that collective work is almost obliged to miss' (Brook, 1968:35). The issue is how the notion of that authorship is privileged, and whether it becomes too deterministic in its ideas of the ownership of meaning.

When THE ACTOR in *The Messingkauf Dialogues* (Brecht, 1965:54) asks, 'Aren't I bound hand and foot by the author's text?', THE PHILOSOPHER replies that 'You could treat the text as a report which is authentic, but has several meanings . . .'. A view of the text is presented which argues that meanings are not actually encoded into the drama text by a writer in order for a company of actors, director, designer and so on to present them faithfully as 'the writer's meanings' – a view which stands contrary to many current, but traditional, critical perceptions. Barbara Izard and Clara Hieronymus in their study of Faulkner, *Requiem for a Nun* write:

> A play comes to life only when it is performed. A play is printed words, a piece of stage literature, until it is spanked into breath by the joint efforts of a cast and an audience, brought to squalling reality and a claim upon actual existence through the birth pangs of its opening night in the theatre. (Izard and Hieronymus, 1970:1)

This is a view which is challenged because it sees meaning as belonging *only* to the writer. More than that, it sees meaning as belonging *only* to a particular semiotic system – writing. A more effective position for critical practice, I would argue, is one that suggests that there is no fixed meaning which is 'brought to life' in production. Meanings differ according to different, though often related, semiotic systems. The according of prime status to one system only is untenable. Intentions to mean in one system should not be used as a means of privileging meanings in another system.

Can we, then, ever know 'the truth'? I would suggest not, because arguments about the importance of intentions suppose that intentions are permanent, whereas they are, like all readings, subject to variability. Just as a reader cannot speak on behalf of a writer's intentions, so writers cannot speak on behalf of their own intentions as fixed, stable and unchanging. Muriel Bradbrook, for example, described the experiences of writer Ann Jellicoe when she saw a number of different productions of *The Knack* (1962) like this:

When she attended her own play in Cambridge she thought it was funny; when she attended it in Bath she thought it was obscene and was shocked; when she attended it in London she thought it was young and innocent.' (Bradbrook, 1972:45)

What I am talking about, therefore, is variation and multiple meanings and the need to make variability and multiplicity the centre of critical practice, rather than the idea of single, writer-oriented meaning. I am talking about rejecting the idea that meaning is an absolute reality encoded into the text by a writer, and subsequently considered to be a commodity owned exclusively by the writer, and, as a consequence of that, I am talking about rejecting the privileging of both the status of writer and the idea of the text as *L*iterature as the exclusive focus for drama criticism.

Literature

Roman Ingarden (1973) draws a distinction between two different texts which he argues constitute 'a play': the main text and the side-text. The main text is considered to be the words and sentences and the side-text is considered to be items like the stage directions. This distinction is not a particularly useful one in the critical practice of drama because it suggests that verbal language not only has a priority over, but is also separate from, action. It is a view which maintains a privileged status for verbal language and a privileged controlling status for the dramatic text as a literary text. Muriel Bradbrook puts the case for the 'superiority' of verbal language when she writes: 'I presume that everyone would agree that verbal language is the most sophisticated form of language' (Bradbrook, 1972:37), and develops this by writing that: '. . . verbal language is the mark of civilization, the most difficult and most flexible, the most permanent and the most integrative element in the mixed art of the drama' (Bradbrook, 1972:49). But the stage directions, amongst other things like character naming, textual and production histories, critical reception, *mise-en-scène*, and so on, are as much a part of the main text as the words assigned to characters to speak and should not, therefore, be marginalised as 'side-texts'.

The 'sensible' course of action, it seems to me, is not to
marginalise any part of a drama text because performance, particularly production, is not a realisation/instantiation of a literary
work, but is an entirely new 'discursive formation'. Drama analysis needs to recognise that this new formation – this new text –
is not simply a staging of a fully formed text which already exists
in writing *before* performances, but is a quite different semiotic
system which requires a quite different semiotic analysis. Richard
Schechner has recognised this for many years in both his work
as director and drama/theatre theorist. When he directed *The
Tooth of Crime* (Shepard, 1974), for example, there were uneasy
negotiations about the production because Shepard was very
uncertain about the analytic approach being taken. He wrote to
Schechner:

> I got a lot of conflicting feelings and thoughts about the whole
> thing . . . I'm really not trying to pull artistic priority bullshit
> because to me the play stands outside me on its own. It's like
> a kid brother that I wanna protect. (Schechner, 1981:166)

Shepard's protective feelings towards 'his' play were understandable given that he considered the play to be a completed
product able to stand 'on its own', but Schechner pointed out to
him that:

> . . . we must work long and hard *to find our own places within
> the world of your script*. Or, to put it another way, we accept
> your script as *part of an art work yet to be completed*. (Schech-
> ner, 1981:166)

Schechner's point that the written text, no matter how complete a writer might think it to be, is never a completed text is
a very important one and establishes 'the text' as just part of
many possible universes of discourse.

No text is ever completed. It is always meanings in process.
Similarly, no matter how thorough and detailed the performance
processes may be, a production does not complete those processes, it simply creates a new text for a particular time, place
and reception. The process of changing meanings continues from
writing to writing; reading to reading; analysis to analysis;

rehearsal to rehearsal; production to production; reception to reception. The concept of 'page to stage', which has been central in much formal semiotic analysis and traditional criticism implies that the written text is merely 'stage-enacted' with all of its written meanings kept intact. I would argue very strongly against this position because an entirely new text is performed each time – albeit one that might have particular interpretations privileged for a particular production purpose – but nevertheless a new text each time. This means, therefore, that a position which maintains, as Ingarden's does, that:

> . . . we should learn virtually everything that is essential for the given drama from the words that the characters speak. (Ingarden, 1973:209)

is untenable because it accords a status to the writers of those words which assumes that they have fixed into those words all the meanings that would ever be required in order to 'stage' the text.

Graham Hough, a traditional literary critic, represents a view that literary criticism is losing its hold on drama to the extent that what he considers to be the literary nature of dialogue in drama (and hence, for him, the 'value' of drama as literature) is giving way to a more 'popular' and hence, for the elitist Hough, 'less respectable' language. He writes:

> The drama – the serious drama more than the trivial – is receding from literature towards a form where gesture, action and inarticulate half-utterance takes the place of self-subsistent dialogue.' (Anderson, 1980:143)

This is a view which suggests that language – at least complex language – is the property of literature and literary criticism. Gaston Bachelard, a contemporary French philosopher, refers to this attitude as 'a simplex of superiority' (Bachelard, 1964:xxi) and it is still a view which is dominant in critical circles. Richard Nickson with just such an air of superiority in an article discussing television drama writes, '. . . television still opts for some dialogue, and in its suds we founder . . .' (Nickson, 1984:409), suggesting that all television offers is soap opera which will never make the grade of 'good' literature because its dialogue is not sophisticated enough; 'sophisticated', in this case, is defined in terms of traditional literary criteria. This is an elitist, anti-popular culture position which argues for the privileging of particular forms of language/dialogue as 'better' – of greater value in literary terms – than other forms. Drama as 'good' literature for Nickson is produced by people like George Bernard Shaw '. . . an amiable dramatist (who) long ago supplied the supporting observation that indeed his plays are all words' (Nickson, 1984:410). Nickson looks back nostalgically to a '. . . heyday the like of which had not been seen since the flourish of restoration comedy' (Nickson, 1984:410) and which presumably we are not to see again unless 'real' dramatists emerge out of the morass of popular culture. This heyday was in the years 1904–7 when the Royal Court theatre in London was under the leadership of Harley Granville-Barker, and is seen to be so important for drama as 'good' literature because '. . . they helped bring into being such highly textual and superior plays as Shaw's *Major Barbara* and Granville-Barker's *The Voysey Inheritance*' (Nickson, 1984:411).

The nature of the 'textual' is, of course, developed by very particular, and limited, literary criteria. *Man and Superman* (Shaw), for example, has stage directions which are several pages long, '. . . a practice which reveals a highly developed distrust of the stage, and of producers and actors, and by implication, elevates the printed text to an autonomous entity in itself' (Pfister, 1988:14). Shaw condemned the plays of Henry James, and in particular *The Outcry*, by arguing that the language was impossible to perform because it was so unlike 'real' dialogue. He went to a production of *The Outcry* (1917) and wrote later:

> . . . there is a literary language which is perfectly intelligible to the eye, yet utterly unintelligible to the ear even when it is easily speakable by the mouth. (Edel, 1949:765)

and condemned James for writing dialogue which no one could understand – a point Shaw made more forcibly in the intervals by reading passages to his guests who declared that they could not understand a word of it. For example:

GRACE: (*As having taken it all in, though not very much needing now to think it over again, while she raises her eyes.*) I'm sorry indeed, Father, to have done you any wrong; but may I ask whom, in such a connection, you refer to as 'they'?

THEIGN: 'They'? (*Pulled up a moment by the question; but then with a brave, high assurance.*) Why, your own Sister, to begin with – whose interest in what may make for your happiness I suppose you decently recognise; and *his* people, one and all, the delightful old Duchess in particular, who only wanted to be charming to you – and who are as good people, and as pleasant and as clever, as any *others* that are likely to come your way. (*After which, crescendo*) Letting alone, John himself, most amiable of men, about whose merits and claims you appear to have pretended to agree with me, just that you might, when he presumed, poor chap, gallantly to *urge* them, deal him with the more cruel effect that beastly blow on the mouth!

(Edel, 1949:789)

As a piece of writing this would probably seem to most people as clumsy and complex – a style which is hypotactic and difficult to follow, with subordination piling upon subordination; with a great many qualifiers, and with a structure that postpones the main information to the end of clauses. Interestingly, Shaw interprets this as too 'literary' for production, but in many ways I would suggest that this style of writing is much closer to certain speech patterns than either Shaw or many later critics would be prepared to recognise. Shaw confuses one semiotic system – writing – with another – writing as speech – and makes value judgements which I would suggest are not as easily transferred as this.

What may be seen as successful and of value in one semiotic system – literature – is used as the criteria for judging the success and value of a quite different semiotic system – drama production. The tension involved in this transference of criteria is what remains, today, as one of the biggest stumbling blocks to an effective critical practice of drama. According to critics like Nickson, modern actors and directors have no respect for 'the text' as a literary artefact, nor for the central tenet of traditional literary critical belief that meaning is encoded into a text by a writer. 'Roll over, Beethoven', he writes, 'the jaunty notion that an artist's "ideas" are something apart from the very words, the very notes, the very paint he [*sic*] uses, sets the stage for breathtaking collaborations. A new spellbinding director may even now be slouching toward *Lear* or *Hamlet*' (Nickson, 1984:417). How dare such directors, he seems to be saying, be so disrespectful to the literature of drama by creating performances which do not concur with a traditional literary critic's interpretation of 'the meaning' of the text? How dare writers, he seems to be saying, assume themselves to be dramatists when they are writing populist, mass media entertainment?

This attitude is tyrannical because it determines very narrowly what should and should not be considered as literature, and by association, as drama. Such tyranny has surfaced in many ways. For example, one of the problems facing Steven Berkoff in his production of *Hamlet* – facing any actor working with a well-known text – was the already well-formed audience perceptions about the 'To be or not to be' speech:

> *For who would bear the whips and scorns of time*, I ask the audience, as if rhetorically . . . I search their faces, bland and innocent, for an answer and would indeed be shocked to get one. I search their faces in The Hague, in Dusseldorf and in Paris, and the audiences were always the same – politely looking on as if secretly engaged in some rite in which they had been privileged to partake: the world's most famous speech and done in English. They knew that this was *the* one, and they would politely and attentively become very quiet and still, most keen to follow each word and each change of thought. There is a curse on famous speeches that makes what was simple and direct suddenly complex and mysterious – to be riddled with hidden depths to be easily mined, and having secret codes to get to the bottom of it and that will result in revelation. So one has to be all the more simple and clear: direct and honest – that will create the grandest possible effect. (But this is not what I always did . . .) (Berkoff, 1989:94f)

The 'curse' that Berkoff writes about here is multi-faceted. As the American sociologist Erving Goffman points out, we are not only expected to perform, we are expected to perform well, and it is this 'well', and what it means and is expected to mean in many different contexts, that is of crucial interest. For many, in drama criticism, the 'well' is determined by literary criteria, which, for the most part I would suggest, are the least appropriate to use. This has been recognised far longer by some theatre professionals than it has by many academics. Charles Marowitz in *An Othello* (Open Space Theatre, London, June 1972) attempted to 'rescue' the characters of *Othello* from the tyranny of the literary classroom and its 'received', i.e. canonical, interpretations. Marowitz used the issues of black revolution in America, and particularly the thinking of people like Malcolm X and writers like Amiri Baraka (LeRoi Jones) to frame his production. In a memo to the company he wrote:

1. Actors playing in Shakespeare's *Othello* are confronted with a threat when a maverick appears in their midst. All are concerned, but the greatest threat is to the actor playing Othello, for the black actor usurping the role of Iago gradually makes him realize that his performance is an integral political factor in a so-called classic which has been playing in the same way for almost four hundred years.
2. The characters in Shakespeare's play gradually become detached from their context. Characters like Iago, Desdemona and Othello, apart from being *dramatis personae* in Shakespeare's work, are also characters in the received world of literature. In a sense, they are *alienated* by traditions for, so powerfully have they been delineated by the past, they almost exist as characters (personages) in their own right. (Marowitz, 1978:178)

To break those characters out of the received world of literature Marowitz:

. . . started out right from the beginning working to make the most blatant contrast possible between all the kind of motherfucking, shit, white-pussy type phrases that would come into Black American speech, so as to get the maximum conflict between that, the hip contemporary language, and traditional Shakespearean verse. Because one thing that began to emerge during the course of the writing was that there shouldn't be any one set style, nor should there be a simple combination of modern situations and classical situations. One was trying to say something about the black political conflict in America, one was trying to say something about the conceptions that people have of Shakespeare's character Othello, and how that related to contemporary political concerns. And one was also trying to say that the characters themselves from Shakespeare's play, as a result of being around for almost four hundred years, have now detached themselves from their original context, so they're in a sense roaming free in a kind of cultural terrain, and therefore can be appropriated and put into a new context . . .' (Marowitz, 1978:186)

That blatancy resulted in a DUKE played as a white Colonel from the American deep south, CASSIO as a young English subaltern and IAGO as a sardonic jester referring to what it is like to be seen as an Uncle Tom in a white world. Charles Marowitz was involved in an approach to drama which not only rejected the idea that meanings are owned by writers and should be sought for and staged faithfully by actors and director but also the very dominant idea that the best people to find those meanings are people trained in traditional literary analysis. What Marowitz, and others like him, are involved in is a *praxis* which recognises that the discourse of drama criticism and production is not innocent. Critics are not objective neutral observers of someone else's meanings, and actors, directors and audiences are not simply involved in staging and observing those meanings faithfully and uncritically. The theoretical and philosophical underpinnings of their critical practice can never be ignored, though the dominant myth is still that they can be. For drama, that has meant, for many years, the twin tyrannies of the privileged 'literary' text and the privileged author. One of the first moves in breaking away from those tyrannies is to recognise that there is not just one voice involved in constructing meanings, but multiple voices.

Multiple Voices

Keith Allen opens his book *Linguistic Meaning* (1986) with the story of a speaker who enters a packed hall of people and approaches the microphone and opens his mouth ready to speak, only to collapse of a heart attack without uttering a word. Allen makes the crucial point that it is of no consequence at all what the speaker intended to say if it was never uttered and never heard. Language matters ONLY when it is part of a social, and therefore, meaningful, interaction.

The philosopher Ludwig Wittgenstein recognised this when he argued that it is 'Practices (*which*) give words their meaning' (Wittgenstein, 1977:32e). By 'practices' he was referring to the idea that it is USE that determines meaning, and not an intrinsic, context-free, meaning encoded into the words. The term 'practices' is important here. The German word Wittgenstein used was *Die Praxis*, and praxis, I would argue, combining Wittgenstein's arguments about language as use and a Marxist understanding of praxis as human activity which, in the face of institutional oppression and alienation (*Entfremdung*), needs to be radical activity in order to bring about change in the human condition, can be a very effective base on which to build a critical practice. Praxis, and relatedly, language involve social and political interaction and change. A critical understanding of drama praxis, therefore, is also about social interaction and change. Praxis is a process of analysis and action designed to bring about change. Praxis is both the action and process which establishes what we, as people and social institutions, do, and what we do is determined discursively, i.e. by the various means we have of making meaning, among them the use of language. Texts are practices which involve social interaction. And social interaction is about power and change.

More often than not communication depends far less on what the words mean than many people realise. Where meanings are triggered by language those meanings are not intrinsic in the system and structure of language; they are made by people, and more importantly by institutions; in social situations which are always changing. What the words themselves mean are often of less consequence than the discourse strategies and structures

involved, as the exchange between the characters JERRY and
EMMA in *Betrayal* (Pinter, 1978:52f) might demonstrate:

JERRY: . . . I have a family.

EMMA: I have a family too.

JERRY: I know that perfectly well. I might remind you that
your husband is my oldest friend.

EMMA: What do you mean by that?

JERRY: I don't *mean* anything by it.

EMMA: But what are you trying to say by saying that?

JERRY: Jesus. I'm not *trying* to say anything. I've said pre-
cisely what I wanted to say.

EMMA: I see.

What is it about this exchange that could result in a performance that might put EMMA on the attack and JERRY on the
defensive? Conflict between the two characters seems to rest not
on something that has actually been said, but on something that
remains unsaid. There does not appear to be a clearly signalled
difference of opinion between them. What there is is a difference
which seems to rest on uncertainty and ambiguity. What is more
likely to be of importance in understanding and then performing
conflict based on uncertainty, are those aspects of the text which
foreground that uncertainty. That, for the most part, seems to
rest initially on uncertainty of what the demonstrative 'that'
refers to throughout the course of the exchange. JERRY and
EMMA seem to understand quite different things by it, and
therefore what might, in other circumstances, have been an effective cohesive way of tieing the text, and thus the characters,
together, might more effectively be performed as a trigger for
ambiguity and hence conflict between EMMA and JERRY.
JERRY's replacing the demonstrative with the more indefinite
'it' in line 6 might then be used to signal his backing off from
the conflict, but EMMA's repeated use of the stronger demonstrative 'that' in her response keeps up the pressure to the point
where JERRY's response becomes much angrier. Conflict
between the two characters might be understood, and developed,
by following a thread of the discourse – in this case demonstrative
pronouns – throughout the exchange, rather than building up a
picture of that conflict by word meanings only. Conflict is based,

in this reading, not on what is *in* the text (endophoric referencing), but what is referred to, from different points of view by the characters, *outside* the text (exophoric referencing). Similarly, the conflict might be developed further, in performance, by underlining the fronting of the subject pronoun 'I' at the beginning of most of the turns that JERRY and EMMA take in the exchange, establishing a power struggle between them to assert themselves over each other, and, amongst other things, the pointing up of the 'too' which is given end-focus in EMMA's first response to JERRY and by that end-focus asserting EMMA's grounds for equal power status with JERRY.

The praxis involved is understanding how meanings are made rather than what is being said, in order to understand the ways in which the characters can effect some sort of change upon each other. Understanding this means understanding what relations of power are involved, and entails a view of language as interaction which, following an understanding of praxis as radical action, assumes that in any exchange amongst people there is a struggle of multiple voices; a struggle for dominance; a struggle to bring about change.

Language and Action

In his essay 'On Dramatic Style', Sartre (1976:17), talks about the inseparability of theatre, language and action:

> Speech in the theater should express a vow or commitment or a refusal or a moral judgement or a defense of one's rights or a challenge to rights of others, and so be eloquence or a means of carrying out a venture, by a threat, for instance, or a lie or something of the sort; but in no circumstances should it depart from this magic, primitive, and sacred role

where the power of language lies in its performative abilities, like the language of shamans and priests, to do something, and by that doing, change something. He continues:

> . . . that language is a moment in action, as in life, and it is there simply to give orders, defend things, expound feelings

in the form of an argument for the defense (that is, for an active purpose), to persuade or accuse, to demonstrate decisions, to be used in verbal duels, rejections, confessions, and the like. As soon as it ceases to be action, it bores us . . . And this concept of language obviously leads ineluctably to the concept of a language as irreversible as action itself. A real action is irreversible, it becomes more and more radical as it goes on; even if you want to reverse and go back to the start, you cannot, you have to go on to the end. It is the radical movement of action that becomes schematized in theater. (Sartre, 1976:105)

Language, when seen in this light therefore, is not simply a means of representation of already existing realities and meanings. It is a language which by its performance does something and thus, out of that action, creates new meanings and realities. Edward Bond in 'A Note on Dramatic Method' (Bond, 1978:xivf) writes:

Effect no longer follows cause, judgement no longer assesses deed, as they did in the past. Not even imagery works for us as it did in the past. Above all, moral language is caught in the same trap. So it is not easy for contemporary writers to contain experience and moral teaching in myths and stories in the way a more secure, settled society could. The way of telling a story, and the normative use of language, no longer contains an implicit interpretation. While we remain part of our present institutional societies our lives have no meaning and therefore stories about them have no meaning. Stories cannot present their own interpretations, can no longer teach us how they should be understood. The dramatist cannot confront the audience with truth by telling a story. The interpretation is counterfeited by society. Even the normative language we use to survive in capitalist society cannot be used to interpret it, our language is fouled by its involvement in that society just as morality is fouled by religion. This means that our moral sanity is at stake. Nor will a technical language of politics or sociology solve the problem because, although it can analyze realism, it cannot reproduce the appearance of reality on stage. And we certainly do not live in a society where the institutions are strong enough to criticize themselves – or rich enough. We are not like American capitalism, which could finance and profit from films on the wickedness of lynching blacks. It is simply that we have to rewrite human consciousness . . . it is as if a child were trying to speak a new language.

That new language, for Sartre and Bond – and for others – is not simply a language of words which represent reality, but a language which classifies and controls subjects, power, status and role relationships. It is a language of action and change because it is about interaction and praxis. It is a language designed to effect change. It is a language which is about conflict because society is about conflict. The praxis involved is to forge a language for performance which both deconstructs and changes the nature of that conflict, from one which oppresses to one which liberates.

That, of course, is a fairly easy thing to write in a book like this, but a considerably more difficult one to bring about. Nevertheless, it is a central tenet of my position that the praxis involved in bringing about that change is one which has to be foregrounded in the discourse of drama (and that means classrooms and theatres/studios etc.), so that it can be foregrounded in the controlling institutions of society.

ANNA in *The Worlds* (Bond, 1980:25) explains this need for a new, liberating, language in an exchange with TRENCH:

TRENCH: (*trying to explain*) You should be helping to run the world. Not pull it apart. You must have reasons for what you do. Then explain them. Make us listen.

ANNA: We just explained. You read it.

TRENCH: But those – words.

ANNA: Meant nothing to you. This society *can't* explain itself to itself. You understand nothing. Yet the public means of explanation – press, television, theatres, courts, schools, universities – almost everywhere ideas are formed or information is collected is owned in one way or another by people like you. Even our language is owned by you. We have to learn a new language.

Drama praxis is about understanding and changing that life by performing new languages. Performing new languages, in that respect, means recognising that the worlds we live in are discursively and textually determined. The language which TRENCH recognises and understands signals a world quite different to the one ANNA is attempting to make him understand because they are using quite different languages within English. In other words, by performing in different languages they perform quite different worlds. Praxis is about recognising those different worlds and attempting to bring about change in those worlds where there is oppression and injustice. Drama praxis is about doing that in those worlds which use and recognise drama texts as part of the way realities are determined and understood. Bertolt Brecht argued that writing for the theatre basically means '. . . laying bare society's causal network/ showing up the dominant viewpoint as the viewpoint of the dominators/writing from the standpoint of the class which has prepared the broadest solutions for the most pressing problems afflicting human society/emphasising the dynamics of development . . .' (Willett, 1964:109). It is this 'laying bare' – the struggle for power and dominance in order to effect change – which is, in the more focused and narrow field of drama texts, drama praxis.

Meaning should not be restricted simply to what words mean, but to the many levels of meaning involved in language as action; in the social and institutional transactions and interactions of people involved in communication. Most of these meanings never find their way into a dictionary – they are meanings involving body movement, facial expressions, voice quality, speed of delivery. They are also meanings involving social niceties and small talk, and the meanings involved in irony, satire, metaphor and paradox; the meanings involved in the hesitations, false starts and silences of language. The meanings too of the ideological, political, philosophical, social and economic assumptions implicit (or explicit) in interaction; the meanings of classist, racist, colonialist, and sexist oppression; the meanings involved in establishing/opposing status and power relationships amongst people; the meanings involved in conflict and co-operation. These are meanings which form the bulk of the meaning processes and strategies in the way people construct texts and are constructed by texts – the way that realities are constructed in social interaction.

Communication is always about doing something to someone else; always about subjects doing something to objects. But this doing is always changing; it is mobile, and it is this notion of mobility which is a crucial one because it signals that no meanings, no subjects and objects, no people or institutions, no social practices, no processes of doing, are fixed and stable. Meaning is always deferred, never completed; it can be changed because it is never finalised.

Performing Meanings

Steven Berkoff (1989:94) demonstrates this deferring of meaning in an account of his interpretations of the 'To be or not to be' speech in *Hamlet*:

> *To be or not to be*,
> A hard walk downstage, stop and deliver the words as if I had said 'stand and deliver' . . . then lower my voice:
> *that is the question*:
> Sometimes I would find this a way of starting to get over the self-consciousness at the beginning of a purple passage, and so I was in it before the audience had noticed, and then I rested to let them take it in. Other times I might start in very slowly indeed, as a kind of confession of my problem, but always directed to them. If I started it hard and quickly then it would appear to be the apotheosis of many hours of thought – as if bursting through the skin of my thoughts it reveals itself: after all the *Angst* of indecision, life is condensed into *To be or not to be* . . .
> Sometimes it would resemble a dialogue with the audience, as if I was expecting an answer.

There is no single way of performing this speech for Berkoff, either in reading, analysis, rehearsal or production. It is always changeable:

> *To die*,
> Let's look at this one as another possible option. Look at the audience . . . such peace . . . such emptiness . . . expiration of

breath even in the saying of it . . . dying while speaking it! To sleep . . . to sleep? Another nagging thought will always threaten a peaceful one. In the state of *Angst*, whichever way one goes there will always be an alternative. Hamlet is full of alternatives since every act has its opposite in order to define the act itself – so both are necessary to the act. To live is bad, but to die could be worse. We would . . . dream!

And since we dream in sleep – and nightmares at that – then imagine the eternity of nightmares that might arise from an endless sleep. We have had a taste of real sleep which is like a little death, and been plagued by terrible visions, so imagine never being able to turn the bloody thing off. Hamlet argues out of the pain of perpetual *Angst*: . . .

Despite the multiple performance voices here of Berkoff as director, writer, actor, HAMLET and not-HAMLET, they lead to a privileging of one interpretation of the character HAMLET that he '. . . argues out of the pain of perpetual *Angst* . . .'. Much of the analysis is directed towards 'finding' and acting upon a number of textual triggers in order to perform, not so much the words of the soliloquy, but the *Angst* of the character HAMLET. What Berkoff does is to privilege a particular interpretation for a character using that privileging, not as a means of establishing it as the correct interpretation, but as part of a dynamic process of making new and different meanings in each production.

This is a crucial point because it means that there is no such thing as a single unchanging text. For example, the production of *Look Back in Anger* (John Osborne: 8 May 1956), now generally considered to be a turning point in British contemporary theatre, resulted in a number of different reviews, which could on the one hand herald it as '. . . a play of extraordinary importance . . .' (*Financial Times*, 10 May 1956), and on the other as '. . . altogether inadequate. The piece consists largely of angry tirades' (*The Times*, 9 May 1956), or as '. . . a rather muddled first drama . . .' (*Manchester Guardian*, 10 May 1956) and '. . . the best play of its decade . . .' (*The Observer*, 13 May 1956). There are many versions, because there are many realities for this particular production on this particular night, even though it might appear that there is only 'one' play. Thirty three years later in a 1989 production of *Look Back in Anger* at the Lyric Theatre, London, one reviewer, John Peter in *The Sunday Times* (13 August 1989:C7) wrote that as Osborne was approaching his sixtieth birthday '. . . it was about time we got him right'; a view which resulted in a sub-editor's headline which announced that John Peter '. . . reveals what the play is really about'. What that turned out to be was a judgement that 'the play' is not about angry young men on the left or right of British politics, but that it is '. . . a verdict of a young writer on an ageing civilisation.'

But what does my 'it' refer to here? John Peter, like the reviewers before him, did not review the performance of a production on a particular night, but something he, and others, called 'the play', and through that, reviewed 'the writer'. The 'it' is therefore not a performance text at all, but something called 'the play' or 'the writer'. These are very familiar categories, but despite their apparent importance in so much drama criticism and activity, they are, I would suggest, categories which defy anyone to review them. In that respect they defy definition in critical practice and are, therefore, of no value. That does not mean that there is no place for writing and writers in drama praxis – far from it – what it means is that as critical/theoretical categories 'the play' and 'the writer' are beyond analysis. What we can handle with varying degrees of confidence is the concept of drama texts in terms of:

the performance of writing
the performance of reading
the performance of analysis
the performance of rehearsal
the performance of production
the performance of reception.

This presents a view of performance which is considerably wider than many critical theories have so far allowed. It immediately focuses attention on the idea that a written text is only a site or surface for constructing meanings in the performance of writing, reading, analysis, rehearsal, production and reception. This, in turn, raises very important issues about how we treat, theoretically and practically, the status of the pre-production drama text. If actors have a written text in their hands; if students have one on their desks, and designers have one on their drawing boards, whose text is it? The writer's? The actor/student/designer's? If writers have a manuscript published; a text produced, whose is it? The writer's? The publisher's? The person who bought a copy from a bookstore? The director of the production? The theatre, television, film company management? Some of the answers, which we will be looking at in various parts of this book, always create conflict. It is the nature of this conflict which interests me, because conflict is central to praxis, and praxis, for me, is central to a socially and politically responsible critical practice of language and discourse.

Bertolt Brecht talked about the difference between the play on paper and the performance of a production as a 'murderous clash', where the production has to overcome the tyranny of the written text (Willett, 1964:22). The result of that clash of performances (written and production) will necessarily be different for different people, just as, so far, the terms 'text'; 'written text'; 'dramatic text'; 'drama'; 'performance'; 'performance text'; 'production' and so on have meant different things to different people. In developing a theory of language and drama praxis I am specifically concerned with drama texts and their relations to performance in English. Those performances include reading, writing, analysis, rehearsal, production and reception – arenas of critical activity which widen considerably the sort of texts which are usually considered as 'dramatic'.

The question which then has to be answered is what distinguishes a drama text from any other text. My answer is *use*. If a text is used for the performance of reading, writing, analysis, rehearsal, production and reception as a drama text, it becomes a drama text.

What then constitutes drama? My answer is the *desire* to use a text for production. I stress desire, because many uses of a text will not result in production. For example, many classroom practices perform texts as writing, reading, analysis, reception, but less frequently as rehearsal and production. Distinguishing between performance and production is crucial and wherever I use the term performance it signals any, or all, of the six activities of writing, reading, analysis, rehearsal, production and reception. When I use the term production I mean the public performance of a text, with an audience of some description.

The genre of drama is defined not by intrinsic means or by a writing process, but by the social uses which are made of texts – any texts – by various institutions like amateur and professional theatre, teaching, television, film, radio, video, journalism, speech therapy, voice coaching, public speaking, designing, reviewing and so on, in any of the performance processes.

Interpretation

Drama texts are always different. Even if the performance is recorded in writing, on audiotape, film or video tape, the drama text will never be the same because of the editorial decisions made in the recording, because of the different conventions involved in the different performance frames, and because of the different receptions involved, both by the audience and by the performers. There are never two occasions when drama texts, of any description, are the same. British dramatist Harold Pinter writes, for example:

> I hope my plays mean something different to everyone who sees them. They should, because there is never one answer. (Wray, 1970:421).

This is a point which the American literary critic Cleanth Brooks did not subscribe to in his reading of *Macbeth* because he felt that a single, unchanging, meaning could be 'found' for the play, and once found nothing more needed to be done. This is a static rather than a dynamic procedure of interpretation, where meaning becomes a finished product. Brooks argued that *Macbeth* could be understood, as a play, by a single image contained in the following lines:

> a naked new-born babe,
> Striding upon the blast, or heaven's cherubim,
> Hors'd upon the sightless couriers of the air . . .
> (I.vii.21–23)

Richard Hornby objected to this approach. He wrote that while Cleanth Brooks:

> . . . makes an interesting and often ingenious argument, it is hard to grant so much weight in a dramatic work to a single passage of such opacity, which requires five seconds to recite, in a scene that depends for much of its effect on a banquet going on simultaneously in the next room. (Hornby, 1977:18)

The point that Hornby makes is an important one because the literary critic has basically treated a drama text as if it holds a single clue to a single meaning for 'the play', and that this clue is 'hidden' in the words of a single passage. To do as Brooks has done is to reduce the drama text to being simply words on a page and to ignore it *dramaturgically*. Denis Diderot, writing in the mid-eighteenth century, in 'The Paradox of Acting' puts it like this:

> And how can a part be played in the same way by two different actors when, even with the clearest, the most precise, the most forceful of writers, words are no more, and never can be more, than symbols, indicating a thought, a feeling, or an idea; symbols which need action, gesture, intonation, expression, and a whole context of circumstance, to give them their full significance? (Diderot, n.d./1883:5)

To consider a drama text as 'the play' and to assume that it is a single entity rather than a multiplicity of potential performances is to ignore 'the context of circumstance'; is to reduce any critical practice to pointlessness. An audience does not have the time, or the literary skills, to search for a single clue in this way and to relate it to 'the meaning' of 'the play'. Nor would it be appropriate if they did. In this type of literary analysis of drama the audience and a particular production are not considered important, or indeed, relevant. The finding of a single meaning in this way was, and is still, often linked to what is thought to be the intention of the writer. This is then considered to validate the 'discovery'. To do this, however, is to misunderstand the dynamism of creating meanings and to seriously disregard changing contexts of performance. Meaning is always deferred, never

completed. All texts are always new texts, regard
many times, and in what ways, they are performe
Edward Bond, who has fought hard in his wo
away from the tyranny of classical/literary drama a__ ....,
recognises this to a certain extent when he writes:

> My public language, as it lies shrouded by the page, may seem
> to some people to be flat. But it is designed to provoke that
> richer language, in performance, that I think is the red-blood
> of any true [*sic*] culture. Don't think that I am content with
> this almost hidden language. It is totally necessary to capture
> the public language and to learn how to use it with subtlety
> and distinctness, but if it replaces that other language then I
> think we would impoverish our species as much as if we'd
> taken the gloss off a starling or the plumage off a parrot. (Hay
> and Roberts, 1980:189)

Peter Brook makes a similar point in *The Empty Space* when
he writes that '. . . the word is a small visible portion of a
gigantic unseen formation' (Brook, 1968:13). This is also, to
some extent at least, Brecht's position when he writes that
'Proper plays can only be understood when performed' (Willett,
ed., 1964:15), and Harold Pinter's when he writes that in language, '. . . under what is said, another thing is being said'
(Pinter, 1976b:14), where 'The speech we hear is an indication
of the speech we don't hear' (Pinter, 1976b:14). Performances
of writing, reading, analysis, rehearsal, production, reception,
are processes which create new meanings, new texts, new languages. They are not simply presentations/expressions of someone else's – a writer's – language.
British dramatist Howard Brenton reinforces this position in
the published text of *The Romans in Britain* (Brenton, 1980)
with an explanatory note before the title page which reads 'This
is the text of the play on the first day of rehearsal'. What happened after that day is the analysis, rehearsal, production, reception processes which cannot be recorded in the written language
of a play script. It also signals, importantly, that the language
and meanings of the play are not the property of the writer, but
are subject to change – are part of a dynamic process of making
meanings. And this is something we need to explore more fully.

At the beginning of the published text of *Death of a Salesman* (Miller, 1950:11) there is a relatively long introduction, 'setting the scene' as it were. At one point it reads:

> A melody is heard, played upon a flute. It is small and fine, telling of grass and trees and the horizon. The curtain rises. Before us is the Salesman's house. We are aware of towering, angular shapes behind it, surrounding it on all sides. Only the blue light of the sky falls upon the house and forestage; the surrounding area shows an angry glow of orange. As more light appears, we see a solid vault of apartment houses around the small, fragile-seeming home. An air of the dream clings to the place, a dream rising out of reality.

There are a number of questions which might be raised. In what ways can a flute 'tell' of grass, trees and the horizon? What does the 'blue light of the sky' actually look like when it 'falls upon the house and forestage'? How can a glow of orange look 'angry'? And how can 'An air of dream' cling to the place? Supposing a director were to follow these stage directions, what would the result look like? Clearly, there would be many variations from as many directors. There would be multiple readings of what appears to be, but isn't, the 'same' text. Similarly the description of LINDA, the salesman's (WILLY LOMAN) wife as:

> Most often jovial, she has developed an iron repression of her exceptions to Willy's behaviour – she more than loves him, she admires him, as though his mercurial nature, his temper, his massive dreams and little cruelties, served her only as sharp reminders of the turbulent longings within him, longings which she shares but lacks the temperament to utter and follow to their end. (Miller, 1950:12)

must, inevitably, result in a different interpretation every time the character LINDA is performed. There is no absolute and definitive interpretation, because there is no absolute and definitive dramaturgical interpretation of such a description of the character, just as there is no absolute production interpretation.

Multiple interpretations produce multiple realities. Reality, then, is not a permanent unchanging state of affairs; there are many realities determined by many different points of view. When, for example, in the Coda to *Jumpers* (Stoppard, 1972:75), one of the characters objects to the introduction of another character (LORD GREYSTOKE (TARZAN)) because '. . . it has been suggested that you are out of a book', and this appears, therefore, too surrealistic, we have the interesting situation of one fictional character believing that he is real while other characters are fictional. GEORGE, in *Jumpers*, sums up the paradox well when he says, 'How does one know what it is one believes when it's so difficult to know what it is one knows?' (Stoppard, 1972:62). This is rather like the fiction of the cinema which presents moving pictures which are, at one and the same time, moving pictures and 'not moving pictures'. Or like, for example, when Laurence Olivier performed as HAMLET in the 1948 film, he is both HAMLET and not-HAMLET; both Laurence Olivier and not-Laurence Olivier; both husband and not-husband; both bachelor and not-bachelor; both actor and not-actor; both director and not-director. 'The truth', as the character ARCHIE in *Jumpers* asserts, 'is always an interim judgement' (Stoppard, 1972:72).

There are, therefore, many ways of making meaning; many realities and many worlds. Drama praxis is about understanding those many ways, recognising the ideologies involved and calling for change if those ideologies are oppressive. That requires an understanding of the way meanings are constructed discursively, and that in turn results in an awareness of how realities – worlds – are created. A central part of that understanding is how we make meanings in language; how we make sense.

2 Making Sense

Realities and Fictions

Most people assume that things make sense. If they do not
appear to be making sense we do our utmost to make them
sensible. Making things sensible is made possible by relating texts
to a set of enabling conventions. Different enabling conventions
will make different sensibilities and different sensibilities create
different realities/fictions.

Elizabeth Wright (1989:55) recounts a story about a director
of the 'Berliner Ensemble', a theatre company known in particular for producing the work of Bertolt Brecht:

> While working with a drama school in Sweden he conducted
> an experiment in which he asked the least gifted student to
> go onto the stage and do nothing either in the way of acting
> or thinking; the others were to guess what it was that their
> colleague was showing. The curtain was slowly raised and the
> lights were dimmed. There was a very long silence while the
> poor fellow just stood there, doing nothing at all. After some
> five to ten minutes someone began to laugh and the laughter
> carried on for five minutes, followed by a period of deep
> gloom. Eventually the curtain came down and the audience
> was asked to comment on what it had seen. They said they
> had experienced the tragedy of man [*sic passim*] in the age of
> technology, his loneliness and alienation. They admired the
> courage of his resistance, his refusal to compromise, his total
> command of the situation, all splendidly acted. But then they
> had laughed when it became obvious that this completely
> inflexible man, while quite unaware of what was going on
> around him in the city, was making a great show of refusal,

superbly acted. Finally, they had felt great sadness on account of the plight of the individual in Sweden. Whereupon the director told them that nothing at all had been performed.

But a great deal had been performed because audiences construct meanings, despite other peoples' intentions, just as a great deal is performed in a text like *Waiting for Godot* despite the now famous remark made by one critic in a review headed 'The Uneventful Event' that it is 'A play in which nothing happens, *twice*' (*Irish Times*, 18 February 1956:6).

Making things sensible is a major means by which people interact. Tom Stoppard plays with this idea in many texts, but in particular takes it to interesting extremes in *Dogg's Hamlet* (1979). He explores the Wittgensteinian problems of language and language games discussed in *Philosophical Investigations*. If a person is building a platform and calls for a plank, a cube, or a block, for example, can we assume that the words used represent the particular objects the builder receives? It seems to be a reasonable assumption, unless the person supplying the objects knows the exact order of the objects required, so that 'plank' might mean 'first'; 'block', 'next'; 'slab', 'ok'; and 'cube', 'thank you'. As long as there is agreement on what the words signify, no difficulties in communication would be created. The point is that language as representation is always fictional. There are no ontological reasons for words meaning what they are deemed to mean. Stoppard explores this idea, and attempts to teach an audience a different set of meanings for familiar words. For example:

BAKER Afternoons! Phew-cycle racks hardly butter fag ends.
CHARLIE (*Agreeing with him.*) Fag ends likely butter consequential.

(Stoppard, 1979:17)

Stoppard offers a translation in the published text, but of course this would not be available in production. The object of the exercise would be for the audience to construct their own meanings – and these would not necessarily be the same. There are performance and production conventions and actions which would offer possible translations, but the whole point of the exercise is to demonstrate how unstable – how 'unreal' – these conventions actually are.

This notion of enabling conventions is an important one, because the actions which we perform by speech are never done in isolation. There are conventions which enable certain performance routines to be considered 'real' and not fictional. So to promise something or to threaten someone or to christen someone or to name a ship only 'really' works if the conventions that enable it to be done are there. And those conventions are socially and institutionally determined. Depending on the frame, if a teacher in a classroom orders the students to leave the room, there are very good chances that it will happen; if a student orders a teacher to leave the room it is less likely that it will happen.

This distinction between conventions which enable 'realities' to be performed is an interesting one because it establishes their role in performance for signalling how meanings are to be constructed by both speakers/hearers, characters/audience. Most important of all it raises important questions for a theory of language and drama praxis about whether it is useful at all to maintain such a distinction between reality and fiction. It is probably more appropriate not to talk about realities at all, but to talk about differing fictions being considered more suitable and appropriate/acceptable in different contexts, frames and conventions.

Reality is not constant, it is always a fiction because of the different points of view – the different ideologies – determining the way the world is constructed and seen. Much of the work of writer and film director Jean-Luc Godard, for example, might be read as a powerful representation of this inability to be sure about reality as a constant. The audience – the reader of the film – has to interact; has to engage in a dialogue with the film, in order to construct the film as film, and in order to construct meanings for that particular performance. Godard has said that 'life arranges itself' (Godard, 1967:7), but it only does that as part of social interaction, and it is the process of 'arranging' which is a crucial part of how meanings are made by people and institutions. Those meanings do not constitute a fixed, unchanging reality. A segment from the filmscript of *Made in USA* (Jean-Luc Godard, 1967:37f) illustrates this:

WORKMAN: If you like, I'll try to show off with sentences, but I don't like doing it.

BARMAN: And why don't you like showing off with sentences?

WORKMAN: Because sentences are collections of words which make nonsense; it says so in the dictionary.

PAULA: But it also says in the dictionary that a sentence is a collection of words which make complete sense.

WORKMAN: I disagree entirely with your definition.

PAULA: Why?

BARMAN: Yes, why do you disagree with her definition?

WORKMAN: Because a sentence can't be a thing which makes nonsense and makes complete sense at the same time.

BARMAN: Well now you're making things difficult for yourself. Because if you don't want to talk in sentences I won't be able to understand you, and if I can't understand you I won't be able to serve you a drink.

(Barman pours workman another drink)

WORKMAN: All right Barman or Paul, I'll have a try.
The glass is not in my wine.
The barman is in the pocket of the pencil's jacket.
The counter is kicking mademoiselle.
The floor is being stubbed out on the cigarette.
The tables are on the glasses.
The ceiling is hanging from the lamp.
The window is looking at the eyes of the mademoiselle.
I open them and the door sits on the stool.
There are three bars in the telephone.
The coffee is filling up with vodka.
There are four walls round the Cinzano.
And the dictionary has only three windows . . .
One American window and two French windows.
The doors are throwing themselves through the window.
The barman is filling a cigarette with his whisky.
He lights his tap.
I am what you are.

He is not what we are.
They are what you are.
He has got what they have.
They have got what we haven't.

A world is being presented here which, for the most part, relies on an already well-established view of reality. That reality is based on a language which structures the world along syntagmatic and paradigmatic axes of meaning. The basic syntagmatic structure of the language of this text has not been altered at all – there are just different paradigmatic choices which seem to disturb already well-perceived notions of how the world means. We might expect the structure subject/phrasal verb/object in the clause 'the door sits on the stool', but less generally expect that structure to be 'filled' with those particular words, even if the structure is changed to subject/verb/adverbial, depending on how you treat 'sits on'. Our expectations about the way the world works are less likely to be upset by the grammar of this text than by the lexical choices. The conflict that arises in understanding how this text means is a conflict – a dialogue – between a familiar grammar and an unfamiliar lexical choice. But that familiar grammar is not simply a representation of an already existing reality, it is just one of the many ways of constructing a reality. For example, the distinction between transitive and non-transitive verbs is one which signals the difference between verbs taking or not taking objects – and in that respect is about someone or something (subject) doing (verb) something (object) to someone or something (indirect object); for example, 'The barman is filling a cigarette . . .'; 'He lights his tap' and so on. This is a view of the world – a reality – which is constructed as a set of relations amongst subjects and objects, but this is not the only way of constructing reality. In this particular drama text this view of the world as subject/object relations is not under threat (though as we will see later on it can be); what is under threat are what constitutes the subjects and objects – the 'someones' and 'somethings'. And this is a far less fundamental threat to existing ideas of reality than one which rewrites the base grammar.

What is important, then, about a view of reality expressed as disturbed expectations is that it suggests that everything is fictional according to the particular frame it is constructed in. A chair on a stage set is not a 'real' chair but a theatrical representation of a chair, even though it may have come straight from the local furniture showroom. Everything in the set would have to be seen this way, except perhaps for babies and animals. It is relatively straightforward to train a dog on stage, but there is always the chance that it will urinate at some unexpected moment because as a dog it is unaware of the conventions that enable the dog to know that what it is doing is fictional. Like a young baby, the dog would never know that it is 'in' a production. This, of course, is the attraction often for having dogs wandering around a set – people expect them not to behave according to the conventions of production.

In an article called 'The Dog on the Stage: Theatre as Phenomenon', Bert States refers to *Two Gentlemen of Verona* which has a character LAUNCE who has a dog called CRAB. This dog, he suggests, usually steals the show just by being a dog. 'Anything the dog does – ignoring LAUNCE, yawning, wagging its tail – becomes hilarious or 'cute' because it is doglike' (States, 1983:379). But, as States points out, it is not as simple as this. The dog may not be aware of the theatrical frame, but the spectators are. Consequently when the dog yawns, the yawn is likely to be taken as a representation of boredom – a comment by the dog on LAUNCE, other characters, the play, the audience, or whatever. Similarly when the dog wags its tail it is likely to be perceived as representing doggy agreement with something that has been said, particularly if these occurrences come at specific moments where the dog appears to be taking turns in the conversation. For example:

Act II:iii

Enter LAUNCE, *leading a dog*

LAUNCE: Nay, twill be this hour ere I have done weeping; all the kind of the Launces have this very fault. (CRAB *nods*) I have received my proportion, like the prodigious son, and am going with Sir Proteus to the Imperial's court. (CRAB *sits*). I think Crab, my dog, be the sourest-natured dog that lives (CRAB *shakes his head*): mother weeping, my father wailing, my sister crying, our maid howling, our

cat wringing her hands, and all our house in a great perplex-
ity, yet did not this cruel-hearted cur shed one tear (CRAB
rolls on his back, tongue hanging out, looking directly at the
audience wagging his tail): he is a stone, a very pebble stone,
and has no more pity in him than a dog (CRAB *raises an*
ear, stands up, cocks his leg against the set, urinates and
walks off stage giving one final look to the audience before
he exits): a Jew would have wept to have seen our parting.
(*sounds off: dog howling*)

This sort of thing, contrived in my example above of course,
can happen. The action of the dog becomes as much a part of the
language of production as the speeches of the actors – because
audiences can slot both of them, dog and actor, into a theatrical
frame which accommodates the actions of the dog as fictional,
while, at the same time, recognising that anything might happen
because the dog is not a 'real' actor and therefore not a 'real'
character. This is rather similar to Hitchcock making a cameo
appearance in one of his films, or John Mortimer appearing in
one of the television productions of *Rumpole of the Bailey*. The
reality of the fiction is somehow broken, yet it remains intact
because the intrusion of the 'real' is not really the real but a
fictional representation of reality, because of the theatrical, filmic
or video frame in which they are appearing.

Julian Beck and Judith Malina in some of the work they did
for 'The Living Theatre' in the 1960s claimed to be representing
themselves on stage – but they were never the 'real' them, as it
were, they were always a theatrical representation of themselves
– indeed, in any situation, in any frame, this is all we ever are.
The frames differ and so do the fronts and the routines, and
therefore the identities. This is true also of the 'environmental'
theatre of directors like Peter Brook and Richard Schechner
where performances take place in 'real' quarries or with a back-
drop of 'real' mountains. The quarries and mountains always
cease to be 'real' because they are immediately appropriated by
the theatrical frame and theatrical conventions into theatrically
representing 'real' quarries or 'real' mountains. They are now, as
quarries and mountains, like the football stadiums, deconsecrated
churches, circus tents and factories for some of the productions
of Dario Fo, occupying a different performance frame – they are

therefore involved in a different fiction to the one they are usually involved in – which may be as a tourist frame, a sacred place frame, a landmark frame, a work frame, a sports frame and so on. There are always different fictions because there are always different frames. In the television production *No Surrender* (Alan Bleasdale, 1989) even though the characters' names are the 'same' as the actors' names (for example, Joan Turner/JOAN TURNER and Bernard Hill/BERNARD HILL) there are still different fictions operating. Their 'own' names are appropriated in the television drama frame, and are as fictional in that frame as they are in any other.

Bert States makes the point about visiting a zoo where a sign states, 'DINGO: wild dog of Australia', behind which is a dingo in a cage. The animal in the cage is seen not so much as a 'real' dingo, but as a representation of the kind of dingo that you might see if you were in Australia. The zoo frame gives a fictional identity to the dingo as a character DINGO representing 'real' dingos. Dogs, actors and language signify one thing within a particular discourse frame and very often are not expected to signify other things in other frames. As I write this in Australia at the moment a famous cricketer is attempting to stop a programme about his alleged affair with a twenty-year-old woman being put to air. The QC acting for the television station has argued that a public figure has no private life – a situation which suggests that there is only one frame allowed for public figures and that is the fictional one created through a particular public production. Examples of media personalities, film and television actors, sportspeople and so on who are constrained into one public frame are legion here, as are the character interpretations, for example, of Laurence Olivier's HAMLET, RICHARD III and HENRY V, Edith Evans's LADY BRACKNELL and Larry Hagman's J.R., to name just a few.

Ideology

Wole Soyinka recounts a story when he was in Cuba after the revolution. Theatre had developed as a very powerful force. He attended a production in a gym in a military camp and at the point when half the audience appeared to be asleep '. . . a sudden movement took place and it took a fair number of the audience in about two seconds flat to the doors running, others were under their seats – many may have thought Batista was back with an artillery barrage' (Soyinka, 1988:45). What had happened was that a sudden barrage of machine-gun fire had occurred within the theatrical frame which was immediately transferred by many in the audience to the Batista repression frame. The fiction of the theatrical frame momentarily became the reality of the discourse frame of revolution.

The term 'discourse' is important here because constructing texts inevitably involves language and communication, and that in turn involves praxis. Meanings are constructed through praxis and that construction involves differing ideologies, and therefore differing realities. Language does not simply represent a reality external to itself 'out there somewhere'. As William James pointed out over 130 years ago, rather than struggling to discover what 'reality' is, all we can effectively attempt to do is to pose the question, 'Under what circumstances do we think things are real?' (Wilden, 1972:124). And those circumstances, as Peter Berger and Thomas Luckmann have made strikingly clear, are ones which result in a socially constructed reality. This follows early Marxist thinking which argues that consciousness is determined by social being. What is central in this idea is that '. . . human thought is founded in human activity (labour) and in the social relations brought about by this activity' (Berger and Luckmann, 1967:18). It is through the choices that are made in the transactions, interactions and texts of communication that realities are created. This is a materialist view of communication which argues that meaning – reality – has no ontological basis, but is determined by social practices. The choices and the associated communicative/discursive strategies and routines which make up those social practices are what determine the meanings, and these strategies and routines are, in turn, determined by ideology.

There is not, therefore, just one reality to be represented by a neutral innocent language; different discourses create different realities because of different, determining, ideologies. This demands that attention be given not simply to the linguistic structures of language, but also to the discursive strategies of communication; to the context and setting; to social and institutional constraints; to power and status relations, to ideology and to change.

One of the major ways that such change is brought about is by focusing upon language categories which disturb received standards, and upset dominant cultural forces. This is a view of discourse as determining, not simply reflecting, reality, which is an important one. The world is not a single, stable, unchanging, pre-determined entity. The discourse of people in social inter-actions creates many worlds – *universes of discourse* – where realities are always fictional because the universe of discourse in which they are created is always fictional. For example, the characters JACK and HARRY in *Home* (Storey, 1970:9f) spend most of their time talking to each other in what might be seen simply as small talk – phatic exchanges. But to dismiss this as relatively meaningless, as many might do for small talk, would be to mistake the crucial importance such exchanges have in creating a universe of discourse for the participants, and there-fore in creating realities for those participants.

JACK: Harry!
HARRY: Jack.
JACK: Been here long?
HARRY: No. No.
JACK: Mind?
HARRY: Not at all.

(*JACK sits down*)

JACK: Nice to see the sun again.
HARRY: Very.
JACK: Been laid up for a few days.
HARRY: Oh dear.
JACK: Chill. In bed.
HARRY: Oh dear. Still . . . Appreciate the comforts.
JACK: What? . . . You're right. Still . . . Nice to be out.
HARRY: 'Tis.
JACK: Mind?
HARRY: All yours.

(JACK *picks up the paper; gazes at it without unfolding it*)

JACK: Damn bad news.

> HARRY: Yes.
> JACK: Not surprising.
> HARRY: Gets worse before it gets better.
> JACK: 'S right . . . Still . . . Not to grumble.

Their world can be performed as a mutually supportive one; one that can stand counter to the threats and conflict that surrounds them, but it is a textually constructed world, based on simple utterances with very little modification, qualification and subordination. But it might also be performed as a co-operative one where co-operation is understood as a degree of conflict, rather than as an opposite to conflict. For example, there are a number of exchanges each of which is marked by the action of JACK: JACK enters (lines 1–4); JACK signals to a chair (lines 5–6); JACK sits down (lines 7–14); JACK signals to a newspaper (lines 15–16); JACK picks up the newspaper (lines 17–21). Within each of these five exchanges the characters 'stroke' each other with non-threatening language, and their world therefore appears to be non-conflictual. They have an equal number of 'strokes' within each exchange, and so there appears to be no conflict between them. But the discourse is still based on conflict because JACK's actions always put him into a position where he initiates the exchange; he makes the opening moves and in that respect sets the agenda for the exchanges. The power relations are unequal – are always unequal, and therefore the language, though it appears to be co-operative and non-threatening, is in fact structured on a fundamental basis of inequality.

Furthermore, their universe of discourse is determined as a non-threatening world by the phatic exchanges only in the light of the other, more threatening worlds around them, constructed by newspaper discourse and signalled by the newspaper that HARRY has with him and which JACK picks up and comments on with hardly a glance. The newspapers construct a reality which threatens not only their immediate universe of discourse, but the ones they have constructed, and had constructed for them in previous years, and which have helped to determine their own subjectivities. The exchanges seem to be based on a balanced number of similar supporting moves which, until the frame shift in the last exchange, might well be used to establish an order of equality for JACK and HARRY which they do not perceive existing in other discourses around them, but which might well be performed as an unequal relationship with JACK initiating each of the exchanges. Who is in control – JACK or HARRY – is something that would then have to be decided in analysis and rehearsal. Simply initiating the opening moves does not automatically mean that JACK would be in control. What might appear, then, to be a simple single reality for this text, based on an understanding of small talk as phatic, i.e. unthreatening exchange, might, therefore, be too limiting an understanding of how the discourse means.

Illusion

We are therefore talking about the illusion of making sense. For example, in *Boesman and Lena* (Fugard, 1980:260f) LENA is unable to understand the OLD MAN's language (Zhosa):

> LENA: (*Shouting after him*) Go on! Why don't you hit me? There's no white *baases* here to laugh. Does this old thing worry you?
>
> (*Turning back to the old man*)
>
> Look, *Outa*. I want you to look.
>
> (*Showing him the bruises on her arms and face*)
>
> No, not that one . . .
>
> (*Pause*)
>
> Why didn't you laugh? They laughed this morning. They laugh every time.
>
> (*Growing violence*)
>
> What's the matter with you? *Kaffers* laugh at it too. It's *mos* funny. Me! *Ou meid* being *donnered*!
>
> (*Pause . . . she moves away to some small chore at the fire. After this she looks up at the old man, and then goes slowly to him.*)
>
> Wasn't it funny?

(*She moves closer*)

Hey, look at me?

(*He looks at her*)

My name is Lena.

(*She pats herself on the chest. Nothing happens. She tries again, but this time she pats him.*)

Outa . . . you . . . (*patting herself*) . . . Lena . . . me.
OLD MAN: Lena.
LENA: (*Excited*) *Ewe!* Lena!
OLD MAN: Lena.
LENA: (*Softly*). My God!

(*She looks around desperately, then after a quick look in the direction in which Boesman disappeared she goes to the half-finished shelter and fetches one of the bottles of water. She uncorks it and hurries back to the old man.*)

LENA: (*Offering the bottle*) Water. Water! Manzi!
(*She helps him get it to his lips. He drinks. In between mouthfuls he murmurs away in Xhosa. Lena picks up the odd phrase and echoes it . . .* 'Bhomboloza Outa, Bhomboloza' . . . 'Mlomo, ewe mlomo' . . . 'Yes, Outa, dala' . . . *as if she understands him. The whole of the monologue follows this pattern: the old man murmuring intermittently – the occasional phrase or even sentence quite clear – and Lena surrendering herself more and more to the illusion of conversation*)

The illusion of conversation results in an illusion of co-operation. It is an illusion that LENA and OLD MAN are not in conflict – but it is only an illusion. There are competing systems of making meaning here, all of which are in conflict. Recognising those different systems and the resultant conflict means recognising that language is fundamentally based on struggles for privileging specific systems over other systems; specific participants over other participants; specific ideas over other ideas; specific classifications of language over other classifications. For example, JANNINGS and GEORGE in *The Ride Across Lake Constance* (Handke, 1973:14f):

JANNINGS: Have you ever had kidneys *flambé*?
GEORGE: No. Not that I know.
JANNINGS: If you don't know then you haven't had them.
GEORGE: No.
JANNINGS: You're disagreeing with me?
GEORGE: Yes. That is: no. That is: yes, I agree with you.
JANNINGS: In other words, when you mention kidneys *flambé* you talk about something you know nothing about.
GEORGE: That's what I wanted to say.
JANNINGS: And about something one doesn't know, one shouldn't talk, isn't that so?
GEORGE: Indeed.

JANNINGS *makes the appropriate gesture with his hand, turning up his palm in the process.* GEORGE *stares at it, and under the impression that* GEORGE *has found something on the palm* JANNINGS *leaves it like that. The hand now looks as if it is waiting for something – for the cigar box, say. After what has been said just now the hand has the effect of an invitation, so* GEORGE *bends down and puts the box in* JANNING's *hand.*
A brief pause, as if JANNINGS *had expected something else. Then he takes the box with his other hand and puts it on his knee. He looks at his hand which is still extended.*

JANNINGS: That's not what I meant to say with that. It only seemed to me that you had noticed something on my hand. (*He opens the box top with his other hand and offers the box to* GEORGE, *who looks inside.*) Take one.

GEORGE *quickly takes a cigar.* JANNINGS *takes one too.* GEORGE *takes the box from* JANNINGS *and puts it back on the table. Each lights his own cigar. Both lean back and smoke.*

GEORGE: Haven't you noticed anything?
JANNINGS: Speak. (*Pause*) Please go ahead and speak.
GEORGE: Didn't you notice how silly everything suddenly became when we began to talk about 'kidneys *flambé*'? No, not so much suddenly as gradually, the more often we mentioned the kidneys *flambé*. Kidneys *flambé*, kidneys *flambé*,

kidneys *flambé*! And didn't it strike you why the kidneys *flambé* gradually made everything so hair-raisingly silly?

Pause

JANNINGS: Speak.
GEORGE: Because we spoke about something that wasn't visible at the same time. Because we mentioned something that wasn't there at the same time!

Of course, the issue might have little or nothing to do with *kidneys flambé*. Making sense here may have more to do with a dialogue between verbal language, visible objects (cigar box), non-visible objects (kidneys), gestures and what, in other contexts, the signifiers (for example, a hand movement, a phrase, an object) have signified. In other words the dialogue involved is a dialogue between a number of competing systems of signification in both the here and now of the interaction between GEORGE and JANNINGS, and in the textual histories – the intertextualities – of those specific signifiers. We are, therefore, talking about a dialogic relationship which is about the competition between intending to mean and making sense; about the conflict between a supposed ontological base for reality and textually/socially constructed realities; about the here and now of communication and the textual histories of communication; about the illusion of making sense.

Order

Language is a struggle of learning, of controlling others and being controlled by others; of constructing realities and of losing control. But it is also a struggle of articulacy and the alienation that that can bring. YORRY in *Fish in the Sea* (McGrath, 1977:32) faces that struggle:

Comrades, the hour draws near. As the historical crisis of British imperialism matures to the point of irresistible conflict, every so-called debate in parliament becomes in fact a dialogue between the Tory and Labour bankrupts on how to meet the resistance of the working class most effectively. There is no doubt, there can be no doubt at all that the Don Quixotes of Toryism would long ago have impaled themselves on the windmills of working-class militancy if it weren't for the Sancho Panzas of reformism.

(*To audience*) The language was getting a bit more fancy every time I opened my mouth. The funny thing was, the more I said, the more powerful I became as a champion of the workers, the further I got away from them . . .

KASPAR in *Kaspar* (Handke, 1969) goes through sixteen phases of learning how to make sense by language in socially constructed worlds, a process Handke calls 'speech torture' (Handke, 1969:11). From the first phase, where he learns a single sentence, the question is asked whether he can 'begin to do something with this sentence' (Handke, 1969:8) to the last phase where having learnt to construct reality through language the questions are: 'Who is Kaspar now? Kaspar, who is now Kaspar? What is now, Kaspar? What is now Kaspar, Kaspar?' (Handke, 1969:9).

KASPAR, like YORRY, eventually comes to recognise that 'Already with my first sentence I was trapped' (Handke, 1969:96). The tyranny of language is that 'I have been made to speak. I have been sentenced to reality' (Handke, 1969:97); '. . . I finally reached the point where I no longer believed not only words and sentences about snow, but even the snow itself when it lay there in front of me or was falling, I did not believe any more and held it neither for real nor as possible, only because I no longer believed the word snow' (Handke, 1969:93). But there is not just one character KASPAR, there are many. They have been taught the model sentences '. . . with which an orderly person struggles through life' (Handke, 1969:44), and they collapse under the collective weight of them. The ideal world of a cosy linguistic co-operation amongst people based on ideas like: 'I say to myself that everything I say to myself is in order' (Handke, 1969:44) can be demonstrated, as YORRY discovers, to be idealistic, distancing, nonsense. The fear of having no language, and therefore no singular identity, can be translated into the recognition that language is not about an individualised order and harmony born out of co-operation but about a socially constructed reality developed out of chaos and conflict:

> While putting other in order
> you are not as quiet and orderly
> as later on
> when you –
> having been put in order
> yourself by thrashing
> that you've given others –
> want to enjoy
> a well-ordered
> world
> and can enjoy
> such a world
> with an untroubled
> conscience.

(Handke, 1969:75)

What is at stake here is a re-defining of 'order'. Making sense is not a process of 'ordering' the world to function without conflict, but a recognition of the defining nature of that conflict. HOSS in *The Tooth of Crime* (Sam Shepard, 1974:66) puts it well:

HOSS: Now I'm outa control. I'm pulled and pushed from one image to another. Nothin' takes a solid form. Nothin' sure and final. Where do I stand! Where the fuck do I stand!

WILLY, a character in *Painting a Wall* (Lan, 1979:20f) develops this much further in his exchange with SAMSON. They are both painting a wall somewhere in South Africa:

WILLY: You know I been thinking about the way we talk.
SAMSON: Ugh man everybody's got some kind of accent.
WILLY: No not that. All the words. We use so few words and some of them don't even mean nothing anymore.
SAMSON: Words mean something. Of course! If they didn't mean something they wouldn't be words.
WILLY: No shut up man. Let me tell you first.

SAMSON: Okay professor.

WILLY: No man don't be like that. What made me think was your name.

SAMSON: What's wrong with my name?

WILLY: What does it mean?

SAMSON: Samson's from the bible. He's the oukie with the hair. You knows the story man.

WILLY: Ja but why not like Samson. So why's you got his name? You not strong like him even.

SAMSON: I have to be called something so people knows who I is. Samson's not my proper name. It's the name I got in school.

WILLY: But it's what you's called now. It's not just your name. It's all names. I'm Willy. What does Willy mean? It's just a word.

SAMSON: It means you.

WILLY: But it doesn't tell you who I *is* at all. Look, when we talk we say 'man', you know. We say 'man'. We say I'm very hungry man. What does that 'man' mean?

SAMSON: It doesn't mean nothing.

WILLY: Why say it then? It's stupid. Like ol'Henry says 'You know' all the time. I just fell down you know. I drank up all the paint you know. You don't know what I know you know. It's nonsense man.

SAMSON: So what? It doesn't matter what people say.

WILLY: It matters. Ja. It matters. Words is like – words is like cages you know. Cages.

SAMSON: You said it now. You know, cages.

WILLY: Ugh shit man. This is important. You're too stupid to know something serious if it was shoved right up your nose. What I'm saying is that we don't have our own words what means our own things.

   Even in the English language, even in Afrikaans the words don't belong to us. We can't make them mean anything. Look we say shit. I say it all the time. And I'm not really talking about shit. The only words I know are shit and fuck and I don't mean to talk about fucking either. They's just words that come out but they don't mean nothing so when they's out they's like bars around me – bars what keeps me doing the same things – thinking the same things – not letting me out to grow – to learn new words. Some people speak beautifully. They know lots of words and they's free men. More free than us. I can't go and talk to anyone 'cause all I can say is fuck and shit. That's not enough.

SAMSON: You talking to me.

WILLY: Ugh man. You only know two words also and one of them I don't even think you can do.

I want to learn new things man. I want to have new words. Like I said, the only words I know are paint, brushes and bricks. And fuck and shit. Fucking paint, fucking brush, fucking bricks. Paint shit, brush shit, brick shit. The end of all my information and words.

It's terrible man. I could do anything if I knew the words. Change this country – build a new world. I could. If I could say the right words in the right way so people would understand about me and my life and all that you and you and Henry and his daughter and all of us. If I could use the right words they'd understand man.

But when they ask me I can't answer them. They say why are you late today? And I must make a joke 'cause how can I tell them all what happens in the place where I stay, on the bus, why I'm late, what I did – I can't.

So I joke and they think I'm rude.

But that's not what I want. I want them to understand. Fuck man. It's not difficult. Lots of people can talk. Why not me? Why not hey? Where can I learn? How can I learn if I have to paint this fucking wall all day? Shit man. I'm sick of it. I've had enough. I'm not doing more. This time I'm not. Fuck. I'm not. I'm leaving too. It's not too late. Fuck I'm going. I'm not painting this wall anymore. This fucking bloody shit covered load of rubbish. Fucking shit I hate it. I'm not staying – fuck – fuck shit the fucking thing to hell – fuck it –!

He can't go. He throws himself at the wall as he shouts the last words, pounding his body at the bricks. His speech dries up altogether before he is physically exhausted.
When he is exhausted he falls to the ground and lies there.
SAMSON *watches.*
HENRY *stares away.*

Eventually WILLY *recovers, picks up his brush, paints over the mark he's made.*
They paint in silence for a while.

WILLY needs language to determine his world, his realities, his identity. The language of those in charge of him is inadequate for this – he effectively becomes language-less, expressing himself only in words like 'fuck' and 'shit'. He is oppressed by the language of others and he is searching for a language to liberate himself from an oppression which condemns him to inarticulacy. He only knows himself through the language of oppressors, and he wishes to know himself through the language of liberation. He is trapped by the language of oppression which keeps him silent and therefore docile and non-threatening. Attempting to change that world creates a chaos – demonstrated here by WILLY losing control – but it is exactly that chaos which is needed in order to bring about change. Nothing is stable, and exploiting that instability is a way of effecting change. That is at the root of praxis.

The view of language, discourse and drama which I have presented thus far demands that there is no absolute closure on interpretive options. There is no correct interpretation of a text in order to determine its reality, but a set of interpretive options which are never fixed but which change according to the different ways people have of making sense, and therefore of making realities. The consequence of that is that no text ever remains the same; it is always part of an interactive process. Making sense is about constructing meanings and realities interactively. That interaction inevitably involves the illusion of co-operation, and analysis of that illusion involves recognising that the fundamental base of how meanings are made – how we make sense – is one of conflict.

3 Conflict

Dialogism

Traditionally language has been seen in terms of sounds, and
the way those sounds combine into meaningful units – morphemes, words, phrases, clauses, sentences and discourses.
Increasingly, however, the study of language is turning away
from this rather narrow structural approach to a recognition
that language is about communicative relations and discursive
formations and not just relations amongst linguistic structures.
Discourse is dialogic because it is about fictions; about the awareness of the social and institutional construction of subjectivity.
We are therefore talking about a view of the world which is
based on a dialectical understanding of the role of the relation
of individual and society. Whenever a person uses language, in
whatever mode, it is useful to imagine that there is a set of
quotation marks around the utterance which signal that this is
not original to this person, but is part of a historical process of
making meanings which involves other language and other texts.
This is a crucial point which flies in the face of most contemporary linguistic thinking on originality and creativity in language.
The French philosopher Jacques Derrida talks about language in
these terms as 'citations'. 'Each text,' Derrida writes, 'is a
machine with multiple reading heads for other texts . . .', where
'. .. one text reads another' (Derrida, 1979:107). This is a very
useful image to bear in mind, because it foregrounds the crucial
concept of intertextuality. All texts are many-voiced.

Bakhtin/Voloshinov talk about this as the 'dialogic imperative',
where one meaning – one voice – is able to influence another
meaning, another voice. This is not a 'cosy' non-violent influenc-

ing based on conversational co-operation, but is a violent clash of power.

Goals

Language as a struggle for power amongst multiple meanings is about both control and conflict in interaction. An example might be the exchange between PORTEN and JANNINGS in *The Ride Across Lake Constance* (Handke, 1973:52):

JANNINGS: Why are you grinning?
PORTEN: I'm not grinning. I'm smiling.
JANNINGS: Stop fidgeting!
PORTEN: I'm not fidgeting, I'm making myself comfortable.
JANNINGS: Shut your trap!
PORTEN: I don't have a trap.

which may not simply be a difference of opinion about what JANNINGS is doing, but a struggle for control; for one character to dominate the other; to manipulate the other character in order to achieve a particular individual goal by shifts in lexical meaning ('grinning', fidgeting' and 'trap' meaning quite different things to JANNINGS and PORTEN) and by PORTEN's discourse strategies concentrating on statements and JANNING's on interrogation and command.

   As JANNINGS and PORTEN might demonstrate, participants do not share goals co-operatively; for the most part, they fight to gain their own goal. If this is an uncomfortable view of language and interaction it is so because over the years a view of language as co-operation has developed which suggests that we operate to a number of maxims of co-operation which we try not to break. We attempt to be relevant in what we say; to be efficient in what we say and to be truthful. But this is an idealisation of the nature of interaction which is very hard to maintain because when the 'real' discourse of interaction is matched against the 'ideal', the 'real' is always deviant. Far better, therefore, to theorise language not as perpetually deviant, i.e. in negative, aberrant terms, but as 'normal'. The difference is that 'normal' signifies conflict, in one form or another. Deborah

Tannen, in a different context (1981b:133) gives the following example:

    F: How often does your acting group work?
    M: Do you mean how often we rehearse or how often we
         perform
    F: both

    M (*Laughs uneasily*)

    F: Why are you laughing?
    M: Because of the way you said that.
         It was like a bullet.
         Is that why your marriage broke up?
    F: What?
    M: Because of your aggressiveness?

What appeared to be the start of a reasonably co-operative exchange developed into a decidedly more uncooperative one. Why? We have no way of knowing from the language 'in' the text unless the transcription included considerably more information about the reference to F speaking 'like a bullet'. Tannen explains that what we are not given in this transcript is the pace of speaker F, or information about the variety of English either participant uses. The comment by M about aggressiveness was made because of the fast pace of F's language, though for F, a New York Jew, this pace did not signal aggression at all. What we are dealing with is a discourse shift which moved from a supportive exchange to a challenging exchange, because a particular discourse feature signalled one meaning to one of the participants and a quite different meaning to the other. The conflict arises because of disturbed expectations, for both participants, about the goals of the exchange. This disturbance is not deviant behaviour, but a normal process of interaction.

It is this idea of interacting with someone in order to effect some sort of change upon them that is of central importance to drama praxis. Lakoff and Tannen (1984) examine, in another context, the linguistic routines and strategies of two characters in the filmscript of *Scenes From a Marriage* (Bergman, 1974:206f):

JOHAN and MARIANNE are a married couple.

JOHAN: Hmmm, that's the big difference between you and me. Because I refuse to accept the complete meaninglessness behind the complete awareness. I can't live with that cold light over all my endeavours. If you only knew how I struggle with my meaninglessness. Over and over again I try to cheer myself up by saying that life has the value that you yourself ascribe to it. But that sort of talk is no help to me. I want something to long for. I want something to believe in.

MARIANNE: I don't feel as you do.

JOHAN: No, I realize that.

MARIANNE: Unlike you, I stick it out. And enjoy it. I rely on my common sense. And my feeling. They co-operate. I'm satisfied with both of them. Now that I'm older I have a third co-worker: my experience.

JOHAN: (*Gruff*) You should be a politician.

MARIANNE: (*Serious*) Maybe you're right.

As Lakoff and Tannen (1984:337) point out, the discourse strategies for each character are quite different. JOHAN has long complex sentences, whereas MARIANNE has short simple ones. His words are long and Latinate, hers are short and native. His life is defined in abstract terms, her strategy is to make abstract concepts more concrete. He uses a professional 'distance' and she develops 'a childlike camaraderie'. Their strategies are different and they irritate each other in the film production because of it. It is not so much what they say to each other that irritates them and causes the friction, but the way they say it, the strategies they use, the pragmatics of their conversations.

We need to be dramaturgically aware of conversational strategies in order to understand roles, relationships and discursive meanings, over and beyond the words that are being used; to understand *conversational implicature*, i.e. the level of meaning in interaction beyond what is actually said *in words*. So, for example, in the exchange between NICK and GEORGE in *Who's Afraid of Virginia Woolf* (Albee, 1964:30f):

GEORGE: So . . . you're in the math department, eh?

NICK: No . . . uh, no.

GEORGE: Martha said you were. I think that's what she

said. (*Not too friendly*) What made you decide to be a teacher?

NICK: Oh . . . well, the same things that . . . uh . . . motivated you, I imagine.

GEORGE: What were they?

NICK: (*Formal*) Pardon?

GEORGE: I said, what were they? What were the things that motivated you?

NICK: (*Laughing uneasily*) Well . . . I'm sure I don't know.

GEORGE: You just finished saying that the things that motivated you were the same things that motivated me.

NICK: (*With a little pique*) I said I *imagined* they were.

GEORGE: Oh. (*Off-hand*) Did you? (*Pause*) Well . . .

any tension which might be performed in this exchange is more likely to be caused, not by what they say to each other but by the conflict between their individual goal orientation. Performed as an exchange of challenges determined by each character having a different goal as they move through the exchange, NICK's 'pique' and GEORGE's 'offhand' reaction might be better understood. What turns out to be a crucial piece of information in this exchange, NICK's assertion that he 'imagined' his motivations about teaching were the same as GEORGE's, was in fact postponed until the very end of Nick's response in line 7. Postponing information like this, to the right of the main clause in an utterance, can have the effect of marking it out as important, focused as it is at the end of the clause; but it can also act like a tag, and appear to be much more of a throwaway remark – something which is considered to be much more of an afterthought than it might have been had it been given thematic prominence at the beginning of the clause. The assumption of shared information about their motivations for going into teaching resulted in quite different goals in the exchanges – NICK to establish some sort of solidarity with GEORGE, and GEORGE to question the basis of that goal of solidarity. NICK argues that 'imagine' should have been interpreted as an important end-focused item, whereas GEORGE interprets it as an afterthought. Their different goals are signalled by quite different discursive strategies involving quite different perceptions about the status of shared knowledge. Marilyn Cooper (1987) demonstrates similar things in an analysis of *Betrayal* (Pinter, 1978:37–8), suggesting that what is at issue is not just the status of the shared knowledge (and lack of it) between JERRY and ROBERT but the fact that the conversation works on the basis of individual rather than shared goals:

ROBERT: They say boys are worse than girls.

JERRY: Worse?

ROBERT: Babies. They say boy babies cry more than girl babies.

JERRY: Do they?

ROBERT: You didn't find that to be the case?

JERRY: Uh . . . yes, I think we did. Did you?

ROBERT: Yes. What do you make of it? Why do you think that is?

JERRY: Well, I suppose . . . boys are more anxious.

ROBERT: Boy babies?

JERRY: Yes.

ROBERT: What the hell are they anxious about . . . at their age? Do you think?

JERRY: Well . . . facing the world, I suppose, leaving the womb, all that.

ROBERT: But what about girl babies? They leave the womb too.

JERRY: That's true. It's also true that nobody talks much about girl babies leaving the womb. Do they?

ROBERT: I am prepared to do so.

JERRY: I see. Well, what have you got to say?

ROBERT: I was asking the question.

JERRY: What was it?

ROBERT: Why do you assert that boy babies find leaving the womb more of a problem than girl babies?

JERRY: Have I made such an assertion?

ROBERT: You went on to make a further assertion, to the effect that boy babies are more anxious about facing the world than girl babies.

JERRY: Do you yourself believe that to be the case?

ROBERT: I do, yes.

(*Pause*)

JERRY: Why do you think it is?
ROBERT: I have no answer.

(*Pause*)

JERRY: Do you think it might have something to do with the difference between the sexes?

(*Pause*)

ROBERT: Good God, you're right. That must be it.
(Pinter, 1978:62f)

Cooper makes the point that the way in which ROBERT manages to manipulate JERRY through this exchange is because he leads him into situations which JERRY had not planned himself. ROBERT's discursive strategies are more direct than JERRY's, and the uncertainty created by the lack of shared knowledge on JERRY's part is exploited to the full by ROBERT. The difference between a question and an assertion becomes a crucial issue. What is of interest is that it is not the content of the exchange that is important but the goal-orientation of the discourse; the shared knowledge they have and the strategies of conflict and co-operation.

Co-operation

Penelope Brown and Stephen Levinson develop co-operation strategies in two main ways: rationality and face. Rationality argues that speakers are able to work out, rationally, the means of achieving particular ends, i.e. that they are engaged in purposeful discourse. Face refers to two needs – to be unimpeded, i.e. free to act without hindrance from the other participants in the interaction (negative face), and to be approved of by other participants of the interaction (positive face). What is of particular interest to drama praxis are the strategies which can be used to maintain or threaten the face of other participants, because these strategies signal the degree of co-operation and conflict which characters may be involved in. Susan Zimin (1981:46), for example, as part of a series of role-play experiments on the

relationship between gender and politeness offered the following
scenario:

> You go to see a movie on campus. In the auditorium there
> are only a few seats left. You find one and sit down. You see
> a female classmate who is around the same age as yourself,
> so you wave to her. Then you notice that you dropped some-
> thing in the aisle, and so, leaving your seat a minute later,
> you find that your classmate has taken your seat. Your coat
> is on the floor and there are no more seats left. You want
> your seat back and you feel angry. What will you say to her?

which resulted in a number of texts which differed markedly in
the strategies used to threaten and maintain face. From the one
below which maintains the face of the seat-stealer throughout by
mostly positive politeness strategies signalling in quite direct ways
a measure of co-operation between the participants:

> Excuse me. I see you've mistakenly taken my seat. I left my
> coat on it; and you're in my seat. Would you pass my coat to
> me. I'm just gonna leave.

to:

> Uh, excuse me. I believe you're sitting in my seat. Didn't you
> notice the coat on it when you threw it on the floor? Well,
> really, I'd really like my seat back, and I don't intend to move.
> Will you get out of my seat.

which moves very firmly from positive strategies to negative ones
(where co-operation is rather more indirectly signalled) to a
complete lack of deference where conflict, and not co-operation,
is the chief result.

Bruce Fraser and William Nolen (1981) in a study of deference
strategies ranked the following according to their informants'
perceptions of politeness:

> I'd appreciate it if you'd do that
> will you do that
> would you do that

could you do that
how about doing that
would you mind doing that
why don't you do that
can you do that
won't you do that
I suggest that you do that
couldn't you do that
do that, could you
I would like you to do that
do that, wouldn't you
shouldn't you do that
do that, won't you
that needs to be done
do that, will you
I must ask you to do that
don't you have to do that
do that, couldn't you
can't you do that
do that, can't you
do that
you have to do that

The more conditional the utterance the more polite it was considered to be. Conditional utterances were therefore considered more deferential than indicative ones; interrogatives more deferential than imperatives; positive modals more deferential than negative modals, and so on.

These strategies signal role relationships, and can function as direction signals to participants about the sort of meanings that are being prioritised. Paul Simpson, in an analysis of *The Lesson* (Ionesco, 1958), demonstrates shifts in the interactive relationship between PROFESSOR and PUPIL caused by different politeness strategies available to both participants (Simpson, 1989). The degree to which PROFESSOR uses elaborate negative politeness strategies at the beginning can direct audiences to read him as less powerful than the pupil; less in control, because he is paying particular attention to the face needs of PUPIL. As the text develops, the strategies can change, by him paying less attention to the face needs of PUPIL, and thus audiences can be directed to seeing him as increasingly powerful, and therefore less co-operative, in his control of PUPIL through his control of the discourse. For example:

PROFESSOR: Good morning, good morning . . . You are . . . er . . . I suppose you really are . . . er . . . the new pupil?

(*The pupil turns round briskly and easily, very much the young lady; she gets up and goes towards the Professor, holding out her hand*)

PUPIL: Yes. Sir. Good morning, Sir. You see I came at the right time. I didn't want to be late.

PROFESSOR: Good. yes, that's very good. Thank you. But you shouldn't have hurried too much, you know. I don't know quite how to apologize to you for having kept you waiting . . . I was just finishing . . . you understand, I was just . . . er . . . I do beg your pardon . . . I hope you will forgive me . . .

PUPIL: Oh, but you mustn't, Sir. It's perfectly allright, Sir.

PROFESSOR: My apologies . . . Did you have trouble finding the house?

PUPIL: Not a bit . . . not a little bit. But then I asked the way. Everyone here knows you.

(Ionesco, 1958:5f)

Neither participant threatens the face of the other here. They are both paying considerable attention to the other's face, but PROFESSOR, by using various apology strategies and hedging a lot of his comments, pays so much attention to maintaining the face of PUPIL that he might be seen to have lost control of the situation. This is not likely to be the case in later exchanges when PROFESSOR talks to PUPIL like this:

PROFESSOR: It would be better if you could keep your eyes off the flies, while I'm giving myself all this trouble for you . . . it would help if you tried to be a little more attentive . . . I'm not the one who's taking the partial doctorate . . . I passed mine long ago . . . my *total* doctorate,

in fact . . . *and* my super-total diploma . . . Can't you understand that I'm only trying to help you?

(Ionesco, 1958:30)

As Brown and Levinson point out in detail (1987:65f) we
threaten face in a variety of ways, by putting pressure on, by
orders, requests, suggestions, giving advice, reminders, threats,
warnings, dares, showing contempt, disapproval, complaints, rep-
rimands, insults, contradictions, challenges, ridicule, bringing bad
news, raising taboo topics, being offensive, expressing violent
emotion, apologising, thanking, accepting, excusing, being
unwilling, by confessions, admissions of guilt, loss of control and
so on. They detail forty of these politeness strategies:

1 Noticing and/or attending to the other participant's
   interests, wants or needs.
2 Exaggerating interest or approval of the other participant.
3 Intensifying interest in the other participant.
4 Using in-group language, like slang, jargon, and particular
   address forms.
5 Agreement by raising safe topics like the weather, small
   talk, repetition.
6 Avoiding disagreement.
7 Asserting common ground/presupposing common ground
   and shared values.
8 Jokes.
9 Asserting or presupposing knowledge and concern of the
   other participant's wants or needs.
10 Offers and Promises.
11 Optimism.
12 Inclusive 'we'.
13 Giving or asking for reasons as a way of implying help.
14 Assuming or asserting reciprocity.
15 Fulfilling the other's needs.
16 Indirect speech acts.
17 Questions and hedges.
18 Pessimism.
19 Minimising impositions.
20 Deference.
21 Apologies.

22 Impersonalising intentions.
23 Generalisations.
24 Nominalisation.
25 Indebtedness.
26 Giving Hints.
27 Associations.
28 Presupposing.
29 Understatements.
30 Overstatements.
31 Tautologies.
32 Contradictions.
33 Irony.
34 Metaphors.
35 Rhetorical Questions.
36 Ambiguity.
37 Vagueness.
38 Overgeneralising.
39 Displacement.
40 Ellipsis.

These co-operative strategies keep the conflict at bay by one or more of the participants in an exchange gaining and maintaining power, and minimising the disturbance of interactional co-operation in what Brown and Levinson (1987:231) call the 'interactional balance'. The only problem, of course, is that 'balance' is theorised here in an ideal world of language where participants are motivated to be as polite as possible and to maintain Gricean maxims of co-operation, when in practice we all of us operate in a messy, noisy world of discourse which is far more about conflict than it is about co-operation, because it is far more about struggling for power.

What is involved is what Bakhtin/Voloshinov call *heteroglossia*, that is a multiplicity of voices; a plurality of experiences and meanings. Language is not about single meanings, or single experiences tied to individuals operating ahistorically. Language is about a plurality of experiences which are determined dialogically, i.e. -

The word, directed towards its object, enters into a dialogically agitated and tension-filled environment of alien words, value judgements and accents, weaves in and out of complex inter-relationships, merges with some, recoils from others, intersects with yet a third group: and all this may crucially shape discourse, may leave a trace in all its semantic layers, may complicate its expression and influence its entire stylistic profile. (Bakhtin, 1981:276).

In other words there is a dialogic relationship involved with every utterance in the here and now with the utterances that have preceded it.

Understanding how meanings are made is a process of understanding intertextuality because 'Each word tastes of the context and contexts in which it has lived its socially charged life' (Bakhtin, 1981:293). The production of meaning and the understanding of meaning are necessarily a dialogue with other texts – with history. This is a struggle of forces, where there is always a dominator and a dominated.

Struggle

The characters BIRD and MOONBOOT in *The Real Inspector Hound* (Stoppard, 1968), regularly shift from the frame of country-house murder investigation to the frame of theatre reviewing in much the same way as frame shifts occur amongst the character groupings in *Each in His Own Way* (Pirandello, 1959) where characters are divided between those 'on stage' and 'real' people in the lobby who comment in a variety of ways on 'the play', or the frame shifts of the 'living newspaper' technique (*discorsi/interventi*) of Dario Fo who improvises on the day's events during productions. The results may be humorous, but the humour works not just because of the appropriation of different frames and genres but also because of the recognition of the ideological assumptions, particularly those associated with value systems based on superior/inferior; high culture/low culture polarities which 'come with' those frames and genres. It is those assumptions which are not given directly within the structures of the text, but which are nevertheless triggered by those structures.

In that respect we can talk about the 'tyranny' of one discourse over another and exploiting an intertextual awareness of various categories of talk, and the appropriateness of context is one of the major ways that a large·number of people can be exploited themselves. This may be relatively harmless, for example, in the way that the characters BIRDBOOT and CYNTHIA exploit melodramatic clichés:

> BIRDBOOT: All right! – let us throw off the hollow pretences of the gimcrack codes we live by! Dear Lady, from the first moment I saw you, I felt my whole life changing—
> CYNTHIA: (*breaking free*): We can't go on meeting like this!
>
> (Stoppard, 1968:38)

which develops into an almost verbatim repetition of an earlier exchange CYNTHIA has had with SIMON (Stoppard, 1968:22–3), and which, despite BIRDBOOT's assertion that he will 'throw off the gimcrack codes', signals that they are, in fact, tyrannised by them because they cannot escape them. Similarly, TEACH in *American Buffalo* (Mamet, 1977:54f) might be performed as someone in a contemporary urban business-world frame who is tyrannised by farewell routines because they signal loss of contact:

> TEACH: Anybody wants to get in touch with me, I'm over the hotel.
> DON: Okay.
> TEACH: I'm not the *hotel*, I stepped out for coffee, I'll be back one minute.
> DON: Okay.
> TEACH: And I'll see you around eleven.
> DON: *O'clock.*
> TEACH: *Here.*
> DON: Right.
> TEACH: And don't worry about anything.
> DON: I won't.
> TEACH: I don't want to hear you're worrying about a goddamned thing.
> DON: You won't, Teach . . .
> TEACH: Then I'm going to see you tonight.
> DON: Goddamn right you are.

TEACH: I am seeing you later.
DON: I know.
TEACH: Good-bye.
DON: Good-bye.
TEACH: I want to make one thing plain before I go, Don.
I am not mad at you.
DON: I know.
TEACH: All right, then.
DON: You have a good nap.
TEACH: I will.

(TEACH *exits*)

DON: Fuckin' *business* . . .

This language is not simply representative of a non-linguistic confusion which exists in urban living. That confusion is itself linguistically determined by social institutions which define urban living in terms of conflict, struggle and the tyranny of discourse. The shifts in modality in TEACH's language might be used as signals of uncertainty. At the beginning of the exchange TEACH does not use any modals at all, and ellipts a number of items, particularly prepositions and adverbs: 'I'm not the hotel', 'I'll be back one minute'. This is a language which is sure of itself, not needing qualification, and presenting an image of someone in a hurry, certain of who he is and the world in which he operates. As the exchange develops so does the modification of the language – adverbials of time and place play an increased role; complex verb phrases replace the simple ellipted ones of the opening utterances; auxiliaries and nominal qualifications increase, signalling the possibility of performing TEACH as a man sure of himself in the narrow world of business discourse, but increasingly uncertain of himself away from that world and the contacts and people of that world. The discourse of TEACH and DON might therefore be performed as a conflict between uncertainty and certainty; of contact and the fear of lost contact; represented by their different discourse strategies and language.

A good example of the sort of fragility that this language – all language – creates because of the fundamental conflicts that are involved might be seen in a scene from *Greek* (Berkoff, 1983:35f):

Cafe. Chorus of kitchen cafe menu sounds and phrases.

EDDY: One coffee please and croissant and butter.

WAITRESS: Right. Cream?

EDDY: Please. Where is the butter so I might spread it lavishly and feel its oily smoothness cover the jagged edges of the croissant?

WAITRESS: Ain't got none. There's a plague on.

EDDY: Then why serve me the croissant knowing you had no butter?

WAITRESS: I'll get you something else.

EDDY: I'll have a cheesecake, what's it like?

WAITRESS: Our cheesecakes are all made from the nectar of the gods mixed with the dextrous fingers of a hundred virgins who have been whipped with bullrushes grown by the banks of the ganges.

EDDY: Ok, I'll have one (*she brings it*) . . . I've finished the coffee now and won't have any liquid to wash the cake down with.

WAITRESS: Do you want another coffee?

EDDY: Not want but must not want but have to/ you took so long to bring the cake that I finished the coffee so bring another . . .

WAITRESS: Ok.

EDDY: But bring it before I finish the cheesecake or I'll have nothing to eat with my second cup which I only really want as a masher for the cheesecake.

WAITRESS: Ok. (*to another waitress*) . . . so he came all over your dress . . .

WAITRESS 2: Yeah.

WAITRESS: Dirty bastard.

WAITRESS 2: It was all thick and stringy it took ages to get off/ he was sucking me like a madman when my mum walked in.

WAITRESS: No! What did she say?

WAITRESS 2: Don't forget to do behind her ears/ she always forgets that.

WAITRESS: I wish my mum was understanding like that/ I haven't sucked a juicy cock for ages, have you?

WAITRESS 2:   No, not really, not a big horny stiff thick hot pink one.

WAITRESS: What's the biggest you've ever had?

WAITRESS 2:   Ten inches.

WAITRESS: No!

WAITRESS 2:   Yeah, it was all gnarled like an oak with a great big knob on the end.

WAITRESS: Yeah?

WAITRESS 2:   And when it came, it shot out so much I could have wallpapered the dining room.

EDDY: Where's my fucking coffee? I've nearly finished the cheesecake and then my whole purpose in life at this particular moment in time will be lost/ I'll be drinking hot coffee with nothing to wash it down with.

WAITRESS: Here you are, sorry I forgot you!

EDDY: About fucking time!

WAITRESS: Oh shut your mouth, you complaining heap of rat's shit.

EDDY: I'll come in your eyeballs you putrefying place of army gang bang.

WAITRESS: You couldn't raise a gallop if I plastered my pussy all over your face, you impotent pooftah bum boy and turd bandit.

(*Enter* MANAGER, *her husband*)

MANAGER: What's the matter, that you raise your voice you punk and scum/ fuck off!

EDDY: No-one talks to me like that

MANAGER: I just did

EDDY: I'll erase you from the face of the earth

MANAGER: I'll cook you in a pie and serve you up for dessert

EDDY: I'll tear you all to pieces, rip out your arms and legs and feed them to the pigs

MANAGER: I'll kick you to death and trample all over you/ stab you with carving knives and skin you alive

(*They mime fight*)

EDDY: Hit hurt crunch pain stab jab

MANAGER: Smash hate rip tear asunder render

EDDY: Numb jagged glass gouge out

MANAGER: Chair breakhead split fist splatter splosh crash

EDDY: Explode scream fury strength overpower overcome

MANAGER: Cunt shit filth remorse weakling blood soaked

EDDY: Haemhorrage, rupture and swell. Split and cracklock jawsprung and neck break

MANAGER: Cave-in rib splinter oh the agony the shrewd icepick

EDDY: Testicles torn out eyes gouged and pulled strings snapped socket nail scrapped

MANAGER: Bite swallow suck pull

EDDY: More smash and more power

MANAGER: Weaker and weaker

EDDY: Stronger and stronger

MANAGER: Weak

EDDY: Power

MANAGER: Dying

EDDY: Victor

MANAGER: That's it

EDDY: Tada.

WAITRESS: You killed him/ I never realised words can kill

EDDY: So can looks

WAITRESS: You killed him/ he was my husband

EDDY: I didn't intend to I swear I didn't/ he died of shock

This is an urban situation which, on the surface, may appear to be a simple service encounter which would normally be defined as successful if no conflict occurs. This language is about deconstructing established views of cosy co-operation amongst people, because language itself, like the different registers used by WAITRESS, is conflictual. The praxis involved is one which argues that urban living is not a comfortable, pleasant, existence but one which is fundamentally conflictual, and which is therefore oppressive. The only way to alter that oppression is to use the conflict in order to effect change. Urban living is assumed to 'work' if people co-operate; it becomes problematic when people conflict with each other. Of course, what rarely gets talked about are the people and institutions who define the criteria of 'success'. The less 'threatening' interaction is to individual participants, the less threatening it is perceived to be for the larger, defining, institutions. The exchange in the Department of Employment between CLERK and DIXIE in the television production of *Moonlighter* from the series *Boys From the Blackstuff* (Bleasdale, 1983:55f) might demonstrate that institutional fear of conflict:

CLERK: Right . . . Name?
DIXIE: Thomas Ralph Dean.
CLERK: Age?
DIXIE: Forty-Four.
CLERK: Date of birth?
DIXIE: Twenty-third of the third, nineteen thirty-eight.
CLERK: Where do you reside?
DIXIE: Forty-seven Maryvale, the Hilltree Estate.
CLERK: How long have you resided there?
DIXIE: Fourteen years.
CLERK: Are you resident at any other address?
DIXIE: The Penthouse Suite at the Holiday Inn.
CLERK: Are you resident at any other address?
DIXIE: No.
CLERK: Have you done any work since your last signing on?
DIXIE: No.
CLERK: Is your wife employed in any capacity?
DIXIE: No.
CLERK: Are any other members of your family employed in any capacity?
DIXIE: No.
CLERK: Do you intend to start work before your next signature?
DIXIE: No.
CLERK: Are you sure that you are not employed in any capacity?
DIXIE: Yes.
CLERK: Thank you, Mr Dean.
DIXIE: It's been a privilege and an honour.

(*He goes*)

This is the language of bureaucracy which protects itself by a series of already formulated questions. When it is threatened it responds with a repetition of one of those questions. This is not the language of co-operation but of submission to a system which recognises that urban living is defined more by conflict than by co-operation, and that by drama praxis with texts like this, the institutions which have vested interests in maintaining 'peace' by oppression, can be shown to be essentially self-serving and repressive. Berkoff (1989:11) writes that in the production of *Greek*, for example, they were after:

> . . . a grotesque, surreal, paranoiac view of life such as is conjured up in dreams . . . What we sought for was a critical analysis where we performed what was unreal and not perceivable in everyday life, and expressed drama less through impersonation than through revelation, hoping that a greater degree of reality would be shown by these methods.

It is this 'reality' – the representation of popular culture in non-standard terms in order to demonstrate that this is 'really' the standard, which results in a discourse which is conflictual because the situations of the base culture are conflictual; they are conflictual because they are about people resisting, in one way or another, social control.

Caryl Churchill develops this in *Softcops* (1983:38f) using the image of Jeremy Bentham's invention of the panopticon:

BENTHAM: . . . I spent years on a scheme of my own. Talking to architects, looking at land. I spent thousands of pounds of my own money. My brother thought of it first in Russia to supervise the workers in the dockyards. It's an iron cage, glazed, a glass lantern –

PIERRE: An iron cage?

BENTHAM: A central tower. The workers are not naturally obedient or industrious. But they become so.

PIERRE: The workers gaze up at the iron cage?

BENTHAM: No no, your idea has to be reversed. Let me show you. Imagine for once that you're the prisoner. This is your cell, you can't leave it. This is the central tower and I'm the guard. I'll watch whatever you do day and night.

PIERRE: I just have to sit here?

BENTHAM: Of course in Russia they were doing work.

BENTHAM *goes behind the curtain, which is the central tower.* PIERRE *goes on sitting. Time goes by. He fidgets.*

PIERRE: Mr Bentham? . . . Do you want me to draw some conclusions? It's not comfortable being watched when you can't see the person watching you . . . You get to know each prisoner and you can compare him with the others . . . You know everything that's going on and I don't know at all. I think it's most ingenious, Mr Bentham, an excellent means of control. Without chains, without pain . . . Is there anything else?

BENTHAM: That you don't need to be watched all the time. What matters is that you think you're watched. The guards can come and go. It is, like your display, an optical illusion.

That sort of control, of course, is pervasive in urban living and creates a discourse of conflict because it is alienating in its effects. MRS FORSYTHE, in *Shout Across the River* (Poliakoff, 1979:15) might be performed as representative of such an alienation:

MRS FORSYTHE: (*nervous smile*) I wouldn't be able to go into the middle of London if I was paid a thousand pounds per minute . . . I can't take a bus now at all . . . I have to walk everywhere. Six months ago . . . about six months ago this is just one thing that happened . . . A bus conductor asked me for my fare, this is a tremendously silly story, but it happens to be true. And I said eight p although I knew it might be more – and he said where are you going? He was rather ugly, he had fierce red hair and I LIED to him. I don't know why, and all the time I was in the bus, I thought he was going to come up to me and shout at me, in front of all those people. And it went slowly – the bus – crawling down the road, almost inch by inch, and I could feel him breathing behind me, and when I got out I was shaking like this – (*She hunches her shoulder*) – and I ran all the way home, like the devil was after me. And when I went to bed that night, I felt there was somebody down in the street, outside the window waiting and watching. And I looked outside and I'm SURE it was him. Jangling these coins in his pocket.

Michael Coveney in *The Financial Times* described this as '. . . the dispiriting evidence of fall-out in a consumer society', and Michael Billington in *The Guardian* described it as '. . . the creeping horrors of urban life.' But I would suggest it can be developed much further than this. This is the discourse of people alienated not simply by the frustrations of daily living, but alienated because they are no longer free. They therefore have to lie, because they are forced to live a lie. The praxis involved in understanding and changing that life is one which requires what society is most frightened of – conflict. As LENA in *A Mouthful of Birds* (Churchill and Lan, 1986) says:

Every day is a struggle because I haven't forgotten anything. I remember I enjoyed doing it. It's nice to make someone alive and it's nice to make someone dead. Either way. That power is what I like best in the world. The struggle is every day not to use it.

I am arguing for a theory of language which suggests that it is not simply a neutral apolitical vehicle by which to carry a writer's, actor's or director's meanings. Language through saying, telling, showing, referring, controlling, doing, and so on, is always about action and interaction; always about power and control. Language is not simply a tool of communication (a popular idea still) but a means by which people demonstrate their commitment, in one way or another, to ideologies and ideas; a means by which people communicate not simply the meanings of words but the meanings of the social interaction and the social networks of which they form a part; a means by which people call for and effect change.

This, then, is an understanding of communication not as a 'cosy' co-operation of individuals doing their best to get on with each other, but as a struggle for dominance and control.

4 Control

Classifications

Drama texts, of any description, are not simply representations or expressions of something else, some other semiotic system or text. They are distinct communicative acts aimed at influencing the thoughts and actions of other people. For example, the characters HESTER and JOHNNIE in *Hello and Goodbye* (Fugard, 1966:17f):

HESTER: Do you sit up all night?
JOHNNIE: When he's bad.
HESTER: You said he was beter.
JOHNNIE: He's getting better.
HESTER: So he was bad.
JOHNNIE: Well on the road to recovery.
HESTER: But he *was* . . .
JOHNNIE: We mustn't talk loud.
HESTER: I'm not talking loud.
JOHNNIE: I'm just saying.
HESTER: Well say it when I'm talking loud!
JOHNNIE: You're starting,
HESTER: Oh shit!

It is not just the linguistic choices that are made here which can communicate conflict, but the discursive choices too. The expectation of conflict developed as a result of intertextual knowledge about previous exchanges between JOHNNIE and HESTER (brother and sister) can be worked out by actors in analysis and rehearsal performances. This exchange might be read as simply cross-talk with little else happening, but it might also be read in terms of the status of the characters, the power relations between them; the conflict involved, and so on: in other words the 'semiotic orientation' which determines the way in which the choices that are made, linguistically and discursively, are oriented by, and towards, social situations and ideologies. We make choices in grammar, transitivity, mood, moves, exchanges, acts and so on but these are not innocent choices. Texts are not simply neutral, ideologically uninvolved instances of different registers, but are institutionally determined, with certain registers more dominant than others. This domination can lead to the view, as it has done, that a particular register is not just more appropriate than others in certain contexts, but is more correct than others in all situations. What this does it to oppress other registers. It means a struggle for power which results in ideologically conflicting registers; ideologically different systems of classifying and controlling the world.

These systems of classification and control are not innocent of ideology. To classify a verbal process as a material action constructs a quite different social meaning than classifying it as a mental process. And, contrary to what many people might think, there is 'absolutely' no reason to suppose that such classifications are fixed. In an exchange like:

  SYL: Make some tea Jack
  JACK: All right
  SYL: Thanks

it makes a considerable difference to issues of power, status and control if the moves in the exchange are classified as:

  SYL: Request
  JACK: Accedes
  SYL: Acceptance

rather than:

  SYL: Command
  JACK: Accedes
  SYL: Challenge

because in the first set we are more easily able to construct JACK as dominant because he controls the outcome of the request and SYL reinforces this by an accepting move of thanks, whereas in the second set we might more forcefully construct SYL as in control given that JACK accedes to a command which is followed by a challenging move of thanks. The words 'on paper' are not enough to determine a reading. So, for example, the written text below, from *Traps* (Churchill, 1978:10), does not by itself have the sort of classificational information required to enable any sort of interpretation to be made about the social and political relationship between SYL and JACK; actors and director would have to make decisions which go beyond the words on the page. Those decisions are necessarily critical, i.e. they construct social meanings of power, status and control for all participants of the performance.

SYL *shuffles cards*

SYL: Pick a card.

JACK *picks a card.*

JACK: You can't do that trick.
SYL: Put it back.

JACK *puts it back*
SYL *shuffles the pack.*

SYL: Where in the pack would you like your card to go?
JACK: You're not going to get it right.
SYL: Tell it where to move.
JACK: Tenth from the top.
SYL: We'll just make sure it's not tenth from the top already.

SYL *deals ten cards, showing* JACK *the tenth.*

SYL: Come on, look at it.
JACK: Of course it's not.
SYL: Right then. Tell it to move.

SYL *puts the dealt cards back on top of the pack.*

JACK: Move, card.
SYL: Right, I felt it go. Here we are then. One. Two. Three.
   Four. Five. Six. Seven. Eight. Nine. Ten. Four of hearts.

JACK: Told you.
SYL: Four of hearts.
JACK: Seven of spades.
SYL: Honest? Shit. Look, here it is, the next card.
JACK: You're not magic.
SYL: You still don't know how I did it.
JACK: You didn't do it.
SYL: I can't count, that's all. I did the trick.

SYL *deals patience and plays.*

If the majority of SYL's moves are interpreted as commands and JACK's are seen as acceptances, then the relationship between them could be constructed in a quite different way to one based on requests. Similarly for all the many different types of moves that could be constructed for the verbal processes of this text. What might appear to be a 'friendly' game could be constructed as a very threatening and tense display of a relationship in crisis, or it could be constructed as a demonstration of a successful and supportive relationship. The constructions of meaning 'for' this text do not lie 'within' the text; they will occur as part of a dramaturgical process of reading, analysis, rehearsal, production and reception, i.e. a process involving *how* the text means, rather than what the words might appear to mean.

In a study of Donald McWhinnie's 1959 radio production of *Embers* (Beckett, 1959) Clas Zilliacus (1970:222–3) discusses the length of the radio silences (in seconds) in the following speech:

HENRY: Who is beside me now? *Pause* (3) An old man, blind and foolish. *Pause* (4) My father, back from the dead, to be with me. *Pause* (4) As if he hadn't died. *Pause* (2) No, simply back from the dead, to be with me, in this strange place. *Pause* (5) Can he hear me? *Pause* (3) Yes, he must hear me. Pause (3) To answer me? Pause (3) No, he doesn't answer me. *Pause* (4) Just be with me. *Pause* (5) That sound you hear is the sea. *Pause. Louder.* (3) I say that sound you hear is the sea, we are sitting on the strand. *Pause* (3) I mention it because the sound is so strange, so unlike the sound of the sea, that if you didn't see what it

> was you wouldn't know what it was. *Pause* (5) Hooves!
> *Pause. Louder.* (3) Hooves!
>
> (Beckett, 1959:21)

Forty eight seconds of spoken text are balanced with fifty seconds of pauses – some of them very long in radio performance time, but there is no direct signal in the published drama text of this length of time despite directions of *pause*. In another speech the production time was one minute and twenty two seconds – again a very long time in radio for a relatively shorts-peech:

> HENRY: Little book. (*Pause*) This evening . . . (*Pause*)
> Nothing this evening. (*Pause*) Tomorrow . . . tomorrow . . .
> plumber at nine, then nothing. (*Pause. Puzzled.*) Plumber
> at nine? (*Pause*) Ah yes, the waste. (*Pause*) Words. (*Pause*)
> Saturday . . . nothing. Sunday . . . Sunday . . . nothing all
> day. (*Pause*) Nothing, all day nothing. (*Pause*) All day all
> night nothing. (*Pause*) Not a sound.
>
> (Beckett, 1959:39)

If a character stops speaking in radio, for any length of time, there is a danger that that silence can signal that they are no longer 'there'. 'Reality', in many respects, depends upon signalling that they are 'there' and long silences can easily distract from that. Donald McWhinnie's decisions, for these speeches, were dramaturgical ones, using the drama text, but concentrating for the production not so much on the *what* of the drama text, but on the *how* of performance texts, particularly analysis and production. That 'how' was not encoded in the drama text.

In a similar study, Marjorie Lightfoot (1969:392) examines the Decca recording of a New York production directed by E. Martin Browne (Decca, New York) of *The Cocktail Party* (T. S. Eliot, 1949), with a specific interest in the way the blank verse was stressed. In an academic article the literary critic Denis Donoghue (1959:132) marks the stress as follows:

> ALEX:
>
>   "Ah, // in that case I know what I'll do.
>   I'm going to give you // a little surprise:

> You knów // I'm rather a famous coók.
> I'm going stráight // to your kítchen now
> And I shall prepáre you // a níce little dínner
> Which you can have alóne. // And thén we'll leáve
> you.
> Meánwhile, // you and Péter can go on tálking
> And Í shan't distúrb you. //
> EDWARD:
>   My deár Alex."

that is, as three-stress with a caesura, whereas Lightfoot tran-
scribes the recording according to four-stress and no caesura
'. . . having in mind the dramatic situation, the character of Alex,
and the relative unimportance of what is being said . . .' (Lightfoot, 1969:392):

> ALEX:
>   Áh, in thát case I knów what I'll dó.
>   I'm góing to gíve you a líttle surpríse;
>   You knów, I'm ráther a famous coók.
>   I'm góing stráight to your kítchen now
>   And Í shall prepáre you a níce little dínner
>   Which yoú can have alóne. And thén we'll leáve you.
>   Meánwhile, you and Péter can go ' on tálking
>   And Í shan't distúrb you.
> EDWARD: My deár Álex.

Donoghue's scansion is based on '. . . an example of the verse
line which Eliot has described, a line of varying length and
varying number of syllables . . .' (Donoghue, 1959:132) and
seems to bear no resemblance to the actual performance practice
of this variety of English which Lightfoot argues is a stress-timed
and not a syllable-timed language and therefore makes a four
stress norm more appropriate given that '. . . interpretation of
character and dramatic situation as well as one's personal speech
habits influence a reading' (Lightfoot, 1969:393). Deciding
between three-stress and four-stress is not made in the drama

text – it is a dramaturgical decision determined by and for performance reasons. FATHER in *Six Characters in Search of an Author* (Pirandello, 1954:17) sums it up well:

> But can't you see that here we have the cause of all the trouble! In the use of words! Each one of us has a whole world of things inside him [*sic passim*] . . . And each of us has his own particular world. How can we understand each other if into the words which I speak I put the sense and the value of things as I understand them in myself . . . while at the same time whoever is listening to them inevitably assumes them to have the sense and value that they have for him . . . The sense and value that they have in the world that he has within him.

It is exactly in this area of meaning that many people find themselves unable to describe just what those 'worlds' are, because though we may be aware of the meanings involved we are often unable to say how, why and where these meanings develop. Most of the readers of this book I would imagine at some point or another have said something like 'It wasn't what was said that bothered me so much as the way it was said', but probably would have difficulty describing exactly what it was in 'the way' that became more important than the words. As WINNIE in *Happy Days* (Beckett, 1961:20) says to WILLIE, 'Words fail, there are times when even they fail', and then has to repeat it because WILLIE does not respond. MR WALTERS a character in *Comedians* (Griffiths, 1976:20) says:

> It's not the jokes. It's not the jokes. It's what lies behind 'em. It's the attitude. A real comedian – that's a daring man [*sic passim*]. He dares to see what his listeners shy away from, fear to express. And what he sees is a sort of truth, about people, about their situation, about what hurts or terrifies them, about what's hard, above all, about what they want. A joke releases the tension, says the unsayable, any joke, pretty well. But a true joke, a comedian's joke, has to do more than release tension, it has to liberate the will and the desire, it has to change the situation.

Edward Bond has said that he thinks in images rather than words and it may well be that such images are much stronger in his mind than the words he eventually writes down (Anderson, 1980:148). Similarly Harold Pinter, like Samuel Beckett, has written that what concerns him most are shapes and structures (Wray, 1970:419), and Peter Brook asks:

> Is there another language, just as exacting for the author as a language of words? Is there a language of actions, a language of sounds – a language of words-as-part-of movement, of word-as-lie, word-as-parody, of word-as-rubbish, of word-as-contradiction, of word-shock or word-cry? If we talk of the more-than-literal . . . is this where it lies? (Brook, 1968:49)

Word-Shock

Antonin Artaud searched for just such an alternative 'theatrical', language where:

> Words do not say everything. By their nature and because they are fixed once and for all, they stop and paralyse thought instead of allowing it free play and encouraging it to develop . . . To spoken language I am adding another language and trying to restore its old magical efficacity, its power of enchantment, which is integral to words, whose mysterious potential has been forgotten. (Hayman, 1977:81)

The language that he added presents certain problems to actors. For example, how do the actors playing BEATRICE and LUCRETIA in *The Cenci* (Artaud, 1964:241) conduct an exchange where one says '!!!!!!!!!!!' and the other replies '!!!!!!!!!!!'? Labelle (1972:387) writes, 'At such a moment the actors must use their own sensitivity and acquaintance with life and cosmos to express what words cannot', not an easy instruction to give an actor.

Artaud was searching for a theatrical language that was much more physical than words which consists of 'everything that occupies the stage, everything that can be manifested and expressed materially on a stage and that is addressed first of all to the senses instead of being addressed primarily to the mind as is the language of words' (Artaud, 1958:38).

Artaud's fear of 'the dictatorship of words' inevitably led him, and others, to a position which gave a prominence, in the making of dramatic meaning, to directors and actors – a prominence which had normally been reserved for writers only, and which in many circles still is. For example, Russell Twisk in the *Observer* (9 July 1989:41) on John le Carré reading his book *The Russia House* on BBC Radio, writes that 'Le Carré reveals a hidden ambition to be an actor. There's novelty in hearing him get his tongue around phoney accents, playing women's voices, confusing, twisting and deceiving us, in an entirely new way. But it's a gimmick. A professional actor with nothing more in his [sic] head but the author's words would have brought more to the telling.' Challenging this sort of attitude allowed Artaud to attack the relationship between the act of writing and the act of production which he saw as unneccessarily divisive. Escaping from the dictatorship of the word involved concentrating much more on a theatrical practice involving the totality of the senses and not just the linguistic ones. This resulted in a theatre of shock tactics and resulted in a theatrical language which no longer depended upon dialogue, but in Artaud's words:

> . . . the only language I could use with a public was to take bombs out of my pocket and throw them in its face with a characteristic gesture of aggression. And that blows are the only language I feel capable of speaking. (Hayman, 1977:135)

'Shit on the Spirit' provides an example:

> lo kunduma papa
> da mama
> la mamama
> a papa
> dama
>
> lokin
> a kata
> repara
> o leptura

o ema
lema

o ersti
o pop
erstura

o erstura
o pop
dima

These linguistic shock tactics have been widely used in contemporary theatre and have been very successful in the *grammelot* of Dario Fo. This is an invented, theatrical, language, which draws, carnival-like, from a wide number of language sources in order to create a praxis which demands that privileging high culture (and associated standard languages) be changed. The most effective direct 'English' equivalent of grammelot, is by Gillian Hanna in her 'translation' of *Elizabeth: Almost By Chance a Woman* (Fo, 1987) where she combines elements from numerous British varieties of English, Early Modern English cant, Italian pronunciation and so on:

GROSSLADY: Omelette's. We all savvy it be Omelette's salt on account of he canst not make up his nous box. He dithers and dathers . . . He oughter've sorted it all long since. Excalibured the poxy nuncle pronto when he was down on his mary-bones jabbering prayers in the gospel shop. 'Now I'll excalibur him . . . no, half a mo' . . . dicket to hissen . . .' I'll be doing him a flavour . . . cos he'd mort scusied of tutti his sins, and he'd locomote diretto to paradiso . . . My old man morted stuffoed full of sin and Boom!, locomoted to hell . . . I'll attend till nuncle locomotes into the chamber with mamma mia and they start playing at rantum scantun '. . . And then he sorties the excalibur . . .' No, I willna fadge it today . . . tomorrow . . . we'll see . . . day dopotomorrow . . . I dinna ken . . . mayhap next week . . .' Odds plut and her nails, her oughter've ordinated the whole shebang in the primo scena when the bogey of Omelette's dad poppied up and dicket: 'O-o-om-le-e-e-tte . . .' The bogey dad parleyed an echo like

all proper bogeys . . . 'O-o-o-omle-e-e-ette . . . i-i-it . . . be-
e-e-e- thy-y-y-y-y- nu-u-u-u-ncle . . . he-e-e-e-e- be-e-e-e-e-
the-e-e-e-e- a-a-a-a-ssa-a-assi-i-n . . . mo-o-o-o-ort hi-i-i-
im . . .'

(Fo, 1987:33f)

Hanna provides an appendix which gives a 'clean' set of speeches for DAME GROSSLADY in standard English – not as a
translation, but as a base for others to work on with language
varieties suitable for their own praxis. This particular speech is
an account of HAMLET and his inability to make up his mind.

Fo's work for the most part is based on situations rather than
characterisation and in much of Fo's work it becomes almost
totally impossible to 'translate' the grammelot because the standard rules of grammar, lexis and syntax of a language are sub-
verted in order to focus, as in Fo's own work in Italian, on the
non-standard language varieties of popular, mass, culture. This
should not be dismissed as sub-cultural, but as a theatrical language designed to politicise the issue of different cultures and to
present them not as 'other' but as a part of a mainstream multiple
culture; as an opposition to a singular, elitist privileging of one
minority culture, for example, standard spoken British English.
The exchange between JOYCE and WILSON in the published
edition of the radio text of *The Ruffian on the Stair* (Orton,
1967:15f) might be performed for similar reasons.

WILSON: (*Smiling*) I've come about the room.
JOYCE: I'm afraid there's been a mistake. I've nothing to
   do with allotting rooms. Make your enquiries elsewhere.
WILSON: I'm not coloured. I was brought up in the Home
   Counties.
JOYCE: That doesn't ring a bell with me, I'm afraid.
WILSON: Is that the room?
JOYCE: That's my room.
WILSON: I couldn't share. What rent are you asking?
JOYCE: I'm not asking any.
WILSON: I don't want charity. I'd pay for my room.
JOYCE: You must've come to the wrong door. I'm sorry
   you've been troubled.

(*She tries to close the door, but* WILSON *blocks it with his foot.*)

WILSON: Can I come in? I've walked all the way here.

(*Pause. He smiles*)

JOYCE: Just for a minute.

(*She lets him in and closes the door. He sits down.*)

I'm so busy. I'm run off my feet today.
WILSON: How about a cup of tea? You usually make one about now.

JOYCE *nods. She goes to the sink but is pulled up sharp.*

JOYCE: How do you know?
WILSON: Oh, I pick up all sorts of useful information in my job.
JOYCE: What's that?

(*She pours water from the kettle into the teapot*)

WILSON: I'm a Gents hairdresser . . .
    My brother was in the business too. Until he was involved in an accident.

(*She puts sugar into his tea and milk*)

JOYCE: What happened?
WILSON: A van knocked him down.

(*Joyce pours her own tea*)

JOYCE: Was he tattooed?
WILSON: You've heard of him?
JOYCE: I've heard of his tattoos.

Each exchange starts off in fairly expected ways, but ends with the unexpected. It is this insertion of the linguistically unexpected which can be used to focus attention upon 'normality' (WILSON's reference to being black, JOYCE's reference to tattoos, and so on) and in that focus can deconstruct it. *The Ruffian on the Stairs* opens, for example, with:

JOYCE: Have you got an appointment today?
MIKE: Yes. I'm to be at King's Cross Station at eleven. I'm meeting a man in the toilet.

(Orton, 1967:13)

The words in isolation may not signal a radical variety of language, but the frameshift certainly can. This is a discursive push against the privileging of singular, elitist, cultures and is what makes much contemporary English drama linguistically distinctive and politically important. Steven Berkoff has been, like Dario Fo, working with a theatrical language in some texts which foregrounds this praxis. SYLV, for example, in *East* (Berkoff, 1977:24f):

SYLV: Piss off thou lump. Thou hast no style for me get lost . . . too old . . . too young . . . too slow . . . I'm too trim for thee and move like what you dream about (on good nights) I'm sheer unadulterated pure filth each square inch a raincoat's fantasy – all there swelled full – I am the vision in your head – the fire you use to stoke your old wife's familiar   stoves . . .

where a non-standard language can be performed as a conflictual response, like the work of Joe Orton, Edward Bond, Howard Brenton, Caryl Churchill, to domination by others by foregrounding a very distinctive non-standard variety of language in order to deconstruct and, in some cases, overthrow control.

This can be clearly seen in the use of *tsotsitaal* in contemporary black South African writing. In many ways, apartheid has resulted in an institutional rejection of traditional languages in South Africa and tsotsitaal, an invented black urban language, based on an Afrikaans, sub-cultural dialect, mixed with Soweto English and various dialects of Sotho and other mainstream South African languages, is developing as a language of resistance. Robert Kavanagh (1985:213) gives an example from *Crossroads* (Workshop '71, 1971):

(SEILANENG *saunters up to Peter and accosts him saucily*)

SEILANENG: Hello, Loverboy.

PETER: (*lowering newspaper slightly*) Hello, Dudu. Go
   bjang?
SEILANENG: Ke teng. O kae wena?
PETER: Where you from?
SEILANENG: I'm from Diepkloof.
PETER: Jy jol weer Diepkloof?
SEILANENG: Ya, ke jola le Madubula.
PETER: Moenie jol in Diepkloof. Ouens van da is moegoes.

As Kavanagh points out, the use of languages like this in
'English' drama texts is not for comic effect. It is a political
move to establish the importance of the everyday languages of
the Witwatersrand in public arenas as a form of resistance against
the privileging of the minority languages (English and Afrikaans), and the tyranny that privileging brings.
   There are, of course, many forms of tyranny. DIG and SIN,
characters in *A Night To Make The Angels Weep* (Terson, 1964),
are hunting hares with a ferret – the ferret has just been in the
hole:

SIN: She's in.
DIG: God, she's on them. The one at the back see sticks its
   eyes to the other's ass and the one at the front is up the
   end of the burrer so she can't get them. Still, she'll be on
   their necks. You can feel her, Dos. You can feel the ground
   shaking. They'm bloody trembling, Diz, trembling their
   heads off.

The language of these characters is described by one critic as
'packed with primitive sensuality' because linguistically 'they
dirty their hands in the bowels of the earth and emerge bloodied,
chthonic gods of primitive power' (Elvgren, 1975:179). I doubt,
if the characters had language which was clearly signalled as
'standard', stockbroker-belt southern English, Elvgren would
have written in this way. Why? Because there has grown up over
many years an association between high culture and 'sophistication' with a written standard English – a literary English, and
therefore a literary sophistication. Deviations from this are often
thought not just to signal non-standard language, and therefore
non-standard characters, but sub-standard language and there-

fore sub-standard, unsophisticated, lacking-in-culture, characters. The idea of the 'literary' carries with it ideas of high and low culture; ideas of superior/inferior relations.

Sam Shepard, like Heathcote Williams and other American writers, has fought hard to overcome this sort of oppressive register dominance by exploring contemporary varieties of American English. WILLIE in *The Unseen Hand* (Shepard, 1975) is a 'spacefreak' and BLUE 'an old juicer':

BLUE: What's with you, boy?
WILLIE: The latitudinal's got us. Now! Now! Smoke it up! Smoke him! Gyration forty zero two nodes! Two nodes! You got the wrong node! Wrong! Correction! Correct that! Step! Stop it! Modulate eighty y's west! Keep it west! Don't let up the field rays! Keep it steady on! . . .

(Shepard, 1975:54)

CISCO is an old friend of BLUE and speaks an 'All right. Now you hold yer fire there while I get out a' my poncho' variety of language (Shepard, 1975:55). He joins BLUE and after a short while:

(*A drunken high school cheerleader kid comes on yelling. He has a blond crewcut and a long cheerleader's sweater with a huge 'A' printed on it. He holds a huge megaphone to his lips. His pants are pulled down around his ankles . . .*)

KID: You motherfuckers are dead! You're as good as dead! Just wait till Friday night! We're going to wipe your asses off the map! There won't even be an Arcadia High left! You think you're all so fuckin' bitchin' just 'cause your daddies are rich! Just 'cause your old man gives you a fuckin' full-blown Corvette for Christmas and a credit card! . . .

(Shepard, 1975:60)

These are varieties of language which stand counter to the dominant culture – not because they are necessarily minority languages or because they belong to specific sub-cultures, but because they threaten the determined standards. SADIE in *AC/DC* (Williams, 1972:136f) for example:

FUCKIN PARA-PIERCING VIBESURGE . . .
THEY'RE FUCKIN YOU IN YOUR THIRD EYE NOW
  PEROWNE . . .
I MEAN THE STIFFEST E.S.P. RIFF EVER BLOW!
DOUBLE EUPHORIA HEAD!
PLAY IT . . . PLAY IT . . . RELAY IT . . . RELAY IT!
GET INTO THEIR ASSEMBLY LANGUAGE. LAY IT
  OUT FOR ME! YOU GOT IT
YOU'RE HITTING IT . . . HITTING IT!
GET INTO THEIR ASSEMBLY LANGUAGE!
LAY IT OUT FOR ME

Similarly in *The Tooth of Crime* (Shepard, 1974) HOSS, an
ageing Elvis Presley-style singer and CROW, a Rolling Stones,
Keith Richards lookalike, engage in a battle of language styles,
the field, mode and tenor of which are all tied to the language
of contemporary, popular, culture. Everything they say, and in
every way they say it, threatens, often by being sexually explicit,
the dominant 'standard' language and culture.

> HOSS: Ya know I had a feeling you were comin' this way.
>   A sense. I was onto a Gypsy pattern early yesterday. Even
>   conjured going that way myself.
> CROW: Cold, Leathers. Very icy. Back seat nights. Tuck
>   and roll pillow time. You got fur on the skin in this trunk.
> HOSS: Yeah, yeah. I'm just gettin' bored I guess. I want
>   out.
> CROW: I pattern a conflict to that line. The animal says no.
>   The blood won't go the route. Re-do me right or wrong?
> HOSS: Right I guess. Can't you back the language up, man.
>   I'm too old to follow the flash.
> CROW: Choose an argot Leathers. Singles or LPs. 45, 78,
>   33⅓.
>
> (Shepard, 1974:46)

As the blurb on the published edition of *AC/DC* puts it, a new
theatrical language is forged in order to explore '. . . the
unnamed and unarticulated contracts that exist between human
beings in dialogue . . .'. It is a question of exploring roles within

a battle of styles in order to establish non-standard identities as normal:

> CROW: Comin' in a wet dream. Pissin' on the pillow. Naked on a pillow. Naked in a bedroom. Baked in a bathroom. Beatin' meat to the face in a mirror. Beatin' it raw. Beatin' till the blood come. Pissin' blood on the floor. Hidin' dirty pictures. Hide 'em from his Ma. Hide 'em from his Pa. Hide 'em from the teacher.
>
> HOSS: Never did happen! You got a high heel. Step to the lisp. Counter you, never me. Back steppin' Crow Bait. History don't cut it. History's in the pocket.
>
> (Shepard 1974:55)

in order to highlight the conflict between standard and non-standard; marked and unmarked discourse.

In the opening of Scene Three of *The Emperor Jones* (O'Neill, 1922:172f) there is a marked contrast between the language of the published stage directions and the language of the main character JONES:

> *Nine o'clock. In the forest. The moon has just risen. Its beams, drifting through the canopy of leaves, make a barely perceptible, suffused, eerie glow. A dense low wall of underbrush and creepers is in the nearer foreground, fencing in a small triangular clearing. Beyond this is the massed blackness of the forest like an encompassing barrier. A path is dimly discerned leading down to the clearing from the left, rear, and winding away from it again towards the right. As the scene opens nothing can be distinctly made out . . . The heavy, plodding footsteps of someone approaching along the trail from the left are heard and Jones' voice, pitched in a slightly higher key and strained in a cheering effort to overcome its own tremors.*
>
> JONES: De moon's rizen. Does you heah dat, nigger? You gits more light from dis forrard. No mo' buttin' yo' fool head again' de trunks an' scratchin' de hide off yo' legs in de bushes. Now you sees whar you'se gwine. So cheer up! From now on you has it easy.

The standard American written English of the stage directions contrasts markedly with the language of JONES. For the theatre of its time of writing, the language of the directions would have been the language of most of the characters (apart from those signalled for comic effect) – their language would not have been marked, therefore, as distinct or threatening. JONES's language, on the other hand, contrasts with this unmarked, standard language, and is very clearly marked as different. It is in this marking that an institutionally determined standard can be disturbed, and in that disturbance call for change. It is of little political concern that the language O'Neill developed at this time may not have accurately represented the specific variety of language he was aiming for; what is of more importance is that the language variety, stereotyped as it may be, reached an American public unused to hearing it as part of its mainstream culture. The mix of singular and plural forms, double negatives, first and second pronouns with third-person forms, clear pronunciation differences, and so on, enable the importance of language as a mix of varieties to be presented by establishing one language as marked against another.

So for example in *All God's Chillun Got Wings* (O'Neill, 1925) there are distinct differences set up between the language varieties of black and white characters, by a very simple differentiation, much along the lines of the tu/vous distinction in French, or the thou/you distinction in Early Modern English (and some contemporary Northern British English dialects and American Quaker English), by distinguishing characters who say *you* or *yo* and *yuh* and *yer*. These are not innocent distinctions made 'simply' to distinguish the language varieties of the different characters, they are political markers of status and power.

The Iceman Cometh (O'Neill, 1947) establishes thirteen different dialects and speech levels amongst the characters in a bar with different status and power relationships. LARRY and PARRITT might be distinguished by the difference between simple (paratactic) utterances and complex (hypotactic) utterances:

LARRY: . . . Well, that's why I quite the Movement, if it leaves you any wiser. At any rate, you see it had nothing to do with your mother.

PARRITT: (*smiles almost mockingly*) Oh, sure, I see. But

I'll bet your mother has always thought it was on her account. You know her, Larry. To hear her go on sometimes, you'd think she was the Movement.

LARRY: (*stares at him, puzzled and repelled – sharply*) That's a hell of a way for you to talk, after what happened to her!

PARRITT: (*at once confused and guilty*) Don't get me wrong. I wasn't sneering, Larry. Only kidding. I've said the same thing to her lots of times to kid her. But you're right. I know I shouldn't now. I keep forgetting she's in jail. It doesn't seem real. I can't believe it's about her. She's always been so free. I – – But I don't want to think of it. (LARRY *is moved to a puzzled pity in spite of himself.* PARRITT *changes the subject.*) What have you been doing all the years since you left – the Coast, Larry?

LARRY: (*sardonically*) Nothing I could help doing. If I don't believe in the Movement, I don't believe in anything else either, especially not the State. I've refused to become a useful member of its society. I've been a philosophical drunken bum, and proud of it. (*Abruptly his tone sharpens with resentful warning.*) Listen to me. I hope you've deduced that I've my own reason for answering the impertinent questions of a stranger, for that's all you are to me. I have a strong hunch you've come here expecting something of me. I'm warning you, at the start, so there'll be no misunderstanding, that I've nothing left to give, and I want to be left alone, and I'll thank you to keep your life to yourself. I feel you're looking for some answer to something. I have no answer to give anyone, not even myself. Unless you can call what Heine wrote in his poem to morphene an answer. (*He quotes a translation of the closing couplet sardonically*)

'Lo sleep is good; better is death; in sooth,
The best of all were never to be born.'

PARRITT: (*shrinks a bit frightenedly*) That's the hell of an answer. (*Then with a forced grin of bravado.*) Still, you never know when it might come in handy.

(*He looks away*)

(O'Neill, 1967:32–3)

PARRITT might be seen as oppressing LARRY with his longer, more complex, utterances; by changing tones of voice; by directives like 'listen to me'; by a more complex vocabulary and by literary quotation. How an actor playing PARRITT performs the last line, of course, will make a big difference as to whether the oppression is seen to be successful or not. A dramaturgical decision would have to be made to determine whether LARRY regains the ground PARRITT has taken from him by his discourse. That decision would involve the assigning of a marked/unmarked category to either LARRY's or PARRITT's discourse.

There are many other attempts to change attitudes by subversion of the standard language. In *Motherlode* (Lawrence Ferlinghetti) language is reduced to half-finished phrases and simultaneous monologues to create confusion – a process of *dépouillement* – a stripping away of language to demonstrate communication as struggle; as conflict; as non-rational. Similarly, *Humanity* (Walter Hasenclever), for example:

Cemetery
Sunset. A cross falls down.

ALEXANDER *rises from the grave.*
THE MURDERER *comes with a sack.*
ALEXANDER *startled.*
THE MURDERER: I have killed!
  Hands him the sack.
  ALEXANDER *stretches out his hand.*

THE MURDERER: The head is in the sack.
  Goes toward the grave, climbs in.
  ALEXANDER *throws dirt over him.*

  A gust of wind.
  The chapel becomes bright.

THE YOUTH. THE GIRL.
THE YOUTH: Who's there?
THE GIRL: A corpse.
  Faints.
THE YOUTH: Murderer!
ALEXANDER: Your coat.

THE YOUTH *takes the coat off his shoulders.*
ALEXANDER *covers himself.*
THE YOUTH: Who are you?
ALEXANDER: I am alive.
Takes the sack over his shoulders. Goes.
THE GIRL *awakens.*
THE YOUTH *embraces her.*
THE GIRL *screams.*   I have deceived you!

(Stanton, 1971:406)

This is completed a little later:

Cemetery.
Sunrise

ALEXANDER *enters with the sack.*
THE MURDERER *rises from the grave.*
ALEXANDER *hands him the sack.*
THE MURDERER: The sack is empty.
ALEXANDER *walks to the grave and climbs down.*

The sun rises.

THE MURDERER *spreading out his arms*:   I love!!

End of Fifth Act

(Stanton, 1971:406)

This strips language down to the minimum, and by so doing suggests the possibilities of understanding 'reality' by means of 'surreality'. In a similar vein is *Rosencrantz and Guildenstern are Dead* (Stoppard, 1969:36), particularly when GUILDENSTERN is playing the role of young HAMLET and the plot of *Hamlet* is reduced to only a few lines of dialogue concluding with:

ROSENCRANTZ: To sum up: your father, whom you love, dies, you are his heir, you come back to find that hardly was the corpse cold before his young brother popped onto the throne and into his sheets, thereby offending both legal and natural practice. Now why exactly are you behaving in this extraordinary manner?
GUILDENSTERN: I can't imagine.

Stoppard takes this one stage further in *Dogg's Hamlet* where the dialogue and action of *Hamlet* is reduced so that the 'entire' play can be run in either fifteen minutes, or an even more reduced two-minute version. And Henryk Tomaszewski went even further in 1979 and reduced all the language of *Hamlet* to zero so that it runs with no words at all. For a writer like Stoppard the praxis involved here may go no further than easy humour, for others the process of what I have called *dépouillement* is a politically important process of defamiliarisation.

Defamiliarisation

The idea of defamiliarisation is an important one in understanding how meanings are made, and when grounded in an ideological move designed to effect political and social change, like in the alienation praxis (*Verfremdungseffekt*) of Bertolt Brecht, a very powerful means of understanding language can be gained. What is crucial is that the critical practice used to isolate and assess such disturbance/defamiliarisation processes develops as an ideological critical practice. This will thereby allow a movement to be made, within criticism, which does not simply comment on the defamiliarisation as an aesthetic/rhetorical effect, but which demystifies and deconstructs that process in order to demonstrate levels of meaning which otherwise might be unaccounted for. Important in such ideological criticism is the foregrounding of interpretation as dynamic reading formations, always aware of the historical intertextualities which constitute the process of constructing meaning and radical praxis.

HAMM for example in *Endgame* (Beckett, 1958:54) is telling a story and says:

I'll soon have finished with this story.

Pause

Unless I bring in other characters.

Pause

But where will I find them?

Pause

Where would I look for them?

(*Pause. He whistles. Enter Clov.*)

Let us pray to God.

This sort of narratorial 'intervention' is well understood, and is a good illustration of the way in which control of a situation can be gained by disturbing normal expectations. It is a form of defamiliarisation or estrangement, what the Russian Formalists called *ostranenie*, which has the ability to shift the direction of meaning from the familiar to the unfamiliar, thereby foregrounding the unfamiliar in order to effect some sort of discursive change. It is a process which has become something of a commonplace in many texts. It would be rather more defamiliarising, for example, if a television newsreader in a primetime news slot abandoned the prepared script on the autocue, and began to recount the intimate details of a recent personal trauma. Or if, as happens in the following example from Sandra Harris's work on the discourse of Magistrates' Courts, the defendant takes control of the questioning:

MAGISTRATE: I'm putting it to you again – are you going to *make* another offer – uh – uh to discharge this debt
DEFENDANT: Would you in my position
MAGISTRATE: I – I'm not here to answer your questions – you answer *my* question
DEFENDANT: one rule for one and one for another – I presume
MAGISTRATE: can I have an answer to my question – please
MAGISTRATE: the question is – are you prepared to make an offer to the court – to discharge – this debt
DEFENDANT: what sort of minimal offer would be required
MAGISTRATE: it's not a bargaining situation – it's a *straight* question Mr H – can I have the answer
DEFENDANT: well, I'll just pay the court a pound annually

MAGISTRATE: that's not acceptable to us

(Harris, 1984:5)

The situation here is an interesting one because the power relations have been reversed. The defendant is adopting a negotiating role in what is usually considered to be a non-negotiating frame. As a consequence the defendant is in rather more control of the discourse than is 'normal'. It is normally very difficult for defendants to introduce new topics or to respond to a question with another question. They are normally firmly under the control of the magistrate. Harris suggests that magistrates have control not just of the turn taking but more importantly of the propositional content of the discourse. Defendants are rarely allowed either to introduce propositions of their own, or to reject the propositions set up by the magistrate. Questions which appear to be innocently soliciting information are best seen as a means of control, because '. . . through the act of questioning one speaker is able to define the way in which the discourse is to continue, and thus also to define participant relationships along a dimension of power and authority' (Harris, 1984:15). For example:

MAGISTRATE: um – and what is you – what are your three – your children living on and your wife
DEFENDANT: well I do know they uh receive supplementary benefit sir – I realize entirely that it's to me to counterbalance that by paying you know I know
MAGISTRATE: are you paying anything at all
DEFENDANT: no I haven't been able to – at all sir – no I get
MAGISTRATE: are you supporting anyone else
DEFENDANT: not at all – no – I live on my own sir
MAGISTRATE: and how much do you receive then
DEFENDANT: fourteen pounds thirty five
MAGISTRATE: well can't you spare anything of that – for your children – um
DEFENDANT: yes – I would do
MAGISTRATE: when did you last pay – anything

(Harris, 1984:16)

DEFENDANT is never in a position to develop an answer because MAGISTRATE always cuts in with a new question. It is MAGISTRATE who is setting the agenda because it is magistrates who establish the propositions. When DEFENDANT attempts to put up a new proposition it is always cut off before it is completed. The questions by MAGISTRATE enable him/her to establish control of the situation and of DEFENDANT and his/her defence. The questions might best be understood, therefore, as accusations, so that 'are you supporting anyone else' could be read as 'you don't support your ex-wife but you choose to support someone else when your wife should have priority' (Harris, 1984:20). Control is exercised in a number of linguistic ways: chiefly by questions functioning as accusations and by control of the propositional content of language, achieved mainly by one person with higher status not allowing, by interruptions, a person in a less privileged position from stating their case, a situation which is deconstructed in *The Madwoman of Chaillot* (Giraudoux, 1958:55)

THE RAGPICKER: I swear to tell the truth, the whole truth, and nothing but the truth, so help me God.

JOSEPHINE: Nonsense! You're not a witness. You're an attorney. It's your duty to lie, conceal and distort everything, and slander everybody.

THE RAGPICKER: All right. I swear to lie, conceal, and distort everything and slander everybody.

DEELEY in *Old Times* (Pinter, 1971) interacts with KATE mainly through questions, giving performance possibilities of always being in control of KATE by dominating her through language, a strategy KATE can turn back on him from time to time:

DEELEY: Why isn't she married? I mean, why isn't she bringing her husband?

KATE: Ask her.

DEELEY: Do I have to ask her everything?

KATE: Do you want me to ask your questions for you?

DEELEY: No. Not at all.

Pause

KATE: Of course she's married.
DEELEY: How do you know?
KATE: Everyone's married.
DEELEY: Then why isn't she bringing her husband?
KATE: Isn't she?

Pause

DEELEY: Did she mention a husband in her letter?
KATE: No.

(Pinter, 1971:12f)

The norm for DEELEY and KATE's discourse is the adjacency of question:answer which generally gives DEELEY the
control. But this norm can be disturbed, because KATE can
fight back by using DEELEY's own question strategy on him,
which she does twice. At both those moments control of the
discourse can shift from DEELEY to KATE, and it is not without significance that Pinter signals that possibility by suggesting
that the actors pause before continuing the exchange. But after
each pause, DEELEY regains control and therefore the domination of KATE.

Domination

Questions of control are central to an understanding of the role
of language in interaction because they bring to light the relations
of power, status and solidarity which have been ignored in most
linguistic models of communication, but which are fundamental
to the way we can understand how texts mean. For example
ROBERT and JERRY in *Betrayal* (Pinter, 1978:33f):

JERRY *sitting*. ROBERT *standing, with glass*.

JERRY: It's good of you to come.
ROBERT: Not at all.
JERRY: Yes, yes, I know it was difficult . . . I know . . .
   the kids . . .
ROBERT: It's all right. It sounded urgent.
JERRY: Well . . . You found someone, did you?

ROBERT: What?
JERRY: For the kids.
ROBERT: Yes, yes. Honestly. Everything's in order.
Anyway, Charlotte's not a baby.
JERRY: No.

Pause

Are you going to sit down?
ROBERT: Well, I might, yes, in a minute.

Pause

JERRY: Judith's at the hospital. The kids are . . . here . . .
upstairs.
ROBERT: Uh-huh.
JERRY: I must speak to you. It's important.
ROBERT: Speak.
JERRY: Yes.

Pause

ROBERT: You look quite rough.

Pause

What's the trouble?

Pause

It's not about you and Emma, is it?

Pause

I know all about that.
JERRY: Yes. So I've . . . been told.
ROBERT: Ah.

Pause

Well, it's not very important, is it. Been over for years,
hasn't it?
JERRY: It is important.
ROBERT: Really? Why?

JERRY *stands, walks about.*

JERRY: I thought I was going to go mad.

ROBERT: When?

JERRY: This evening. Just now. Wondering whether to phone you. I had to phone you. It took me . . . two hours to phone you. And then you were with the kids . . . I thought I wasn't going to be able to see you . . . I thought I'd go mad. I'm very grateful to you . . . for coming.

ROBERT: Oh for God's sake! Look, what exactly do you want to say?

There are various performance options depending on the level of control and dominance analysts/actors/directors and so on wish to establish for the characters. ROBERT's responses could be handled as challenges to JERRY, and challenge or solidarity could be signalled by the orientation of intonation patterns, pitch, stress, voice levels, voice types, and rhythms of ROBERT's move being mirrored, or changed, in JERRY's response moves. The challenges could be aggressive, or merely inquisitive. ROBERT's first challenge provokes a response from JERRY which might seem to suggest that the 'not at all' was far from encouraging. This could be played very aggressively, as indeed could ROBERT's response to JERRY's 'Yes, yes, I know it was difficult'. Much would depend on the amount of room a director is prepared to negotiate for the character ROBERT to reduce the opportunities for JERRY to manoeuvre in the conversation. Generally speaking, JERRY has to keep opening and re-opening the conversation and in that respect ROBERT is very firmly in control, as even the openings ROBERT offers might well be treated as challenges. Control, for the most part, in this dialogue might best be handled in terms of the degree of challenge and support characters give each other in the moves they are making in the conversation. The less support ROBERT gives JERRY the more he appears to challenge him and therefore the more likely he is to be the most dominant. These roles, of course, could well be reversed – there is nothing intrinsic in the words of the drama text which demand that ROBERT be dominant and JERRY under control.

Deirdre Burton (1980) develops this in some detail using a much expanded model of transaction and exchange which was originally formulated by John Sinclair and Malcolm Coulthard for the analysis of classroom discourse, and shows how, in terms of the exchanges, moves and acts which characters make, one character can gain control. In her analysis of the participant relations in *The Dumb Waiter* (Pinter, 1960) she demonstrates that BEN controls GUS by using more censure moves and a great many more directives (67 against GUS's 4), and when GUS attempts to do the same a considerable amount of conflict is likely. BEN is a 'superior managerial member' while GUS is forced into a 'subservient and inferior role'.

Austin Quigley in an analysis of *The Dwarfs* (Pinter, 1977) makes the important point that 'To control what someone is able to say is to control to a considerable extent what they are able to be' (Quigley, 1974:417). For example:

> PETE: (*briskly*) I've been thinking about you.
> LEN: Oh?
> PETE: Do you know what your trouble is? You're not elastic. There's no elasticity in you. You want to be more elastic.
> LEN: Elastic? Elastic. Yes, you're quite right. Elastic. What are you talking about?
> PETE: Giving up the ghost isn't so much a failure as a tactical error. By elastic I mean being prepared for your own deviations. You don't know where you're going to come out next at the moment. You're like a rotten old shirt. Buck your ideas up. They'll lock you up before you're much older.
> LEN: No. There is a different sky each time I look. The clouds run about in my eye. I can't do it.
> PETE: The apprehension of experience must obviously be dependent upon discrimination if it's to be considered valuable. That's what you lack . . .
>
> (Pinter, 1977:100–101)

PETE can be performed as controlling LEN by concentrating on the registerial differences of their language. PETE might be considered as being in considerably more control of his own language than LEN is of his because PETE demonstrates a fluency which appears to be beyond LEN. This, of course, depends upon a cultural privileging of articulacy being of higher value and status than disfluency. Whoever is able to control that value system is therefore able to control the people who are unable to match its standards. Exploiting the difference between these two levels of linguistic skill means exploiting relations of control and power. LEN reaches a point, for example, where he says to another character MARK:

> LEN: You're trying to buy and sell me. You think I'm a ventriloquist's dummy. You've got me pinned to the wall before I open my mouth. You've got a tab on me, you're buying me out of house and home, you're a calculating bastard. (*Pause*) Answer me. Say something. (*Pause.*) Do you understand? (*Pause.*) You don't agree? (*Pause*) You disagree? (*Pause*) You think I'm mistaken? (*Pause*) But am I? (*Pause*) Both of you bastards, you've made a hole in my side, I can't plug it! (*Pause.*) . . .
>
> (Pinter, 1977:107)

Where LEN seems able to recognise that he has been oppressed linguistically by the 'greater' skills of MARK and PETE he is unable to counter that oppression because, in this exchange, MARK refuses to take the floor and give LEN the linguistic opportunity of gaining control of him. When MARK does engage verbally:

> LEN: Do you believe in God?
> MARK: What?
> LEN: Do you believe in God?
> MARK: Who?
> LEN: God?
> MARK: God?
> LEN: Do you believe in God?
> MARK: Do I believe in God?
> LEN: Yes.
> MARK: Would you say that again?
>
> (Pinter, 1977:111)

he oppresses LEN by never allowing LEN's opening move to be developed beyond re-opening moves. LEN may have interesting things to say; interesting propositions to put on the agenda of the exchange, but MARK persistently blocks them. LEN is trying to understand the world linguistically, but is frustrated in this by MARK and PETE.

If LEN is unable to control language, he is unable to control the people around him: he therefore becomes controllable by others. The characters MARK and PETE define what constitutes coherent language, so much so that LEN can not only be defined in terms of his inability to do things with language, he can also be defined because of his fears of what language, in the hands of other characters, can do to him:

> The fundamental battle is for linguistic dominance, for control of the means by which identity, sanity and reality are created for a given community. The central linguistic issue in the Pinter world is not, as had generally been supposed, one of communication, but one of control. Language has an important role in establishing those normative concepts that define social reality which in turn have a controlling power over individual identity and growth. (Quigley, 1974:421)

Kripa Gautam makes similar points in an analysis of *The Caretaker* (Pinter, 1960) where the main characters MICK, ASTON and DAVIES spend most of their time negotiating role relationships. MICK can assert authority over DAVIES by acting as the linguistic 'superior' in any exchange between them. This can then result in DAVIES being suspicious of any interaction he might have with MICK, for example:

DAVIES: (*vehemently*). I keep to myself, mate. But if anyone starts with me though, they know what they got coming.
MICK: I can believe that.
DAVIES: You do. I been all over, see? You understand my meaning? I don't mind a bit of a joke now and then, but anyone'll tell you..that no one starts anything with me.
MICK: I get what you mean, yes.
DAVIES: I can be pushed so far . . . but . . .
MICK: No further.
DAVIES: That's it.

MICK *sits on the head of* DAVIES *bed.*

What you doing?

MICK: No, I just want to say that . . . I'm very impressed by that.

DAVIES: Eh?

MICK: I'm very impressed by what you've just said.

Pause

Yes, that's impressive, that is.

Pause

I'm impressed, anyway.

DAVIES: You know what I'm talking about, then?

MICK: Yes, I know. I think we understand one another.

DAVIES: Uh? Well . . . I'll tell you . . . I'd . . . I'd like to think that. You been playing me about, you know. I don't know why. I never done you no harm.

MICK: No, you know what it was? We just got off on the wrong foot. That's all it was.

DAVIES: Ay, we did.

(Pinter, 1960:48f)

When DAVIES attempts to gain control, after a history of exchanges where MICK has oppressed him, MICK appears to give him some ground, but displaces him quickly by manipulating DAVIES into believing that they are on equal linguistic footing, but which by the end of the exchange puts MICK well and truly back in control, and both of them back in their original roles.

5 Roles

Routines and Fronts

Jean-Paul Sartre in *Being and Nothingness*:

> Let us consider this waiter in the cafe. His movement is quick
> and forward, a little too precise, a little too rapid. He comes
> toward the patrons with a step a little too quick. He bends
> forward a little too eagerly; his voice, his eyes express an
> interest a little too solicitous for the order of the customer.
> Finally there he returns, trying to imitate in his walk the
> inflexible stiffness of some kind of automaton while carrying
> his tray with the recklessness of a tightrope-walker by putting
> it in a perpetually unstable, perpetually broken equilibrium
> which he perpetually re-establishes by a light movement of the
> arm and head. All his behaviour seems to us a game. He
> applies himself to chaining his movements as if they were
> mechanisms, the one regulating the other; his gestures and
> even his voice seem to be mechanisms; he gives himself the
> quickness and pitiless rapidity of things. He is playing, he is
> amusing himself. But what is he playing? We need not watch
> long before we can explain it; he is playing at being a waiter
> in a cafe. There is nothing there to surprise us. The game is
> a kind of marking out and investigation. The child plays with
> his [*sic*] body in order to explore it, to take inventory of it;
> the waiter in the cafe plays with his condition in order to
> realise it.(Goffman, 1969:66)

As Erving Goffman, who cites the Sartre example, makes
clear, all of us, at every moment of our lives, are performing an
institutionally determined role of some description. When those

108

moments involve interaction with other people then those performances are more publicly ritualised than others, like the roles and fronts we may adopt in a church service, a school classroom, a doctor's surgery, a job interview, an expensive restaurant, a theatre. 'Front' is a term developed by Goffman to describe that part of performance which 'regularly functions in a general and fixed fashion to define the situation for those who observe the performance' (Goffman, 1976:91). We all have a changing number of socially determined fronts which we learn to recognise, manipulate and negotiate with. There is, for each of us, an institutionally determined lexicon of routines and fronts which are socially understood. Learning those routines and fronts, developing others, and recognising the meanings involved, is a crucially important part of interaction, and, most importantly, an integral part of language. It is not simply an innocent, fictional, activity which is linked to 'play-acting' in the theatre or playground, it is a crucial means by which we determine identities (i.e. subjectivity) and by which we interact with others.

Athol Fugard, John Kani and Winston Ntshona develop this particularly well in *Sizwe Bansi is Dead* (1974:38) when the character BUNTU has to teach SIZWE BANSI (MAN) the new role of ROBERT ZWELINZIMA – not for play-acting, but for survival in a South Africa that demanded that all black people carry identifying passbooks which, determined by the white authorities, identify and control the lives of all these black people.

MAN: I'm afraid. How do I get used to Robert? How do I live as another man's ghost?

BUNTU: Wasn't Sizwe Bansi a ghost?

MAN: No!

BUNTU: No? When the white man looked at you at the Labour Bureau what did he see? A man with dignity or a bloody passbook with an N.I. number? Isn't that a ghost? When the white man sees you walk down the street and calls out, 'Hey, John! Come here' . . . to you, *Sizwe Bansi* . . . isn't that a ghost? Or when his little child calls you 'Boy' . . . you a man, circumcised with a wife and four children . . . isn't that a ghost? Stop fooling yourself. All

I'm saying is be a real ghost, if that is what they want, what they've turned us into. Spook them into hell, man!

And after going through a series of role plays in order to get *SIZWE BANSI* used to his new identity as ROBERT ZWELIN-ZIMA BUNTU says:

BUNTU (*angry*) All right! Robert, John, Athol, Winston . . . Shit on names, man! To hell with them if in exchange you can get a piece of bread for your stomach and blanket in winter. Understand me, brother, I'm not saying that pride isn't a way for us. What I'm saying is shit on our pride and we only bluff ourselves that we are men.

Take your name back, Sizwe Bansi, if it's so important to you. But next time you hear a white man say 'John' to you, don't say '*Ja, Baas*?' And next time the bloody white man says to you, a man, 'Boy, come here,' don't run to him and lick his arse like we all do. Face him and tell him: 'White man. I'm a man!' *Ag kak*! We're bluffing ourselves.

It's like my father's hat. Special hat, man! Carefully wrapped in plastic on top of the wardrobe in his room. God help the child who so much as touches it! Sunday it goes on his head, and a man, full of dignity, a man I respect, walks down the street. White man stops him: 'Come here, kaffir!' What does he do?

(*Buntu whips the imaginary hat off his head and crumples it in his hands as he adopts a fawning, servile pose in front of the white man.*)

'What is it, Baas?'

If that is what you call pride, then shit on it! Take mine and give me food for my children.

(*Pause*)

Look, brother, Robert Zwelinzima, that poor bastard out there in the alleyway, if there *are* ghosts, he is smiling tonight. He is here, with us, and he's saying: 'Good luck, Sizwe! I hope it works.' He's a brother, man.

(Fugard *et al.*, 1974:43)

The roles for the black people are determined by the white dominating forces. Identities and subjectivities are not freely chosen. People are determined as subjects/objects by others; by larger, more powerful and dominant social and institutional forces, and it is that determination which decides, for the most part, the roles we perform. Praxis is about changing oppressive determination of such roles.

The socialisation of roles tends to fix perceptions about the performance of roles. Goffman gives the classic example of the sailor returning home from many months at sea in the company of men only, and asking his mother to 'Pass the fucking butter' (Goffman, 1969:12), where one role (and its associated discourse) is considered appropriate by some in one context, and inappropriate in another. In other words there are, for some, fixed perceptions about the role of sailors and mothers which lead to both moral and value judgements being made about the appropriateness of discourse in certain contexts. Deborah Schiffrin (1988:262f), for example, asks of the following two texts:

CUSTOMER: You have coffee to go?
SERVER: Cream and sugar?
CUSTOMER: Yes please.
SERVER: That'll be 50 cents.

   (CUSTOMER *pays 50 cents*)

CUSTOMER: You have 1986 Corvettes?
SERVER: Convertibles?
CUSTOMER: Yes please
SERVER: That'll be $30,000.

   (CUSTOMER *pays $30,000*)

why is the first text more likely to be considered appropriate discourse in a service encounter, and the other not? In the coffee exchange there is an implicit pre-request for a coffee, but not in the Corvette exchange. But how do we recognise that there is an implicit pre-request? It's not 'in' the text. We presumably 'know' because of the shared contextual and intertextual knowledge we have of service encounters like this.

Henry Widdowson, a British educationist/linguist, gives an

example from a book published in New Delhi designed to give model answers for interviewers to learn for production at interviews, which demonstrates quite well how the perceived superiority/inferiority of roles can be disturbed by deconstructing that expected contextual and intertextual knowledge:

Impressive Interview no 26

CHAIRMAN: Good morning Miss Mohoni. Take your seat.
ANSWER: Good morning, sir. Thank you.
CHAIRMAN::   Why are you going for an administrative career?
ANSWER: That I am a woman should by no means militate against the chances of my carving out an administrative career for myself. Women have already figured conspicuously in the various departments of human life and activity. If they could prove accomplished scholars, renowned politicians, consummate administrators and, to crown it all, orators of great repute, there seems no earthly reason why consideration of sex alone should constitute a bar to my building a career for myself. I hope that I shall not have any difficulty in adapting myself to surroundings and atmosphere, not otherwise happy or congenial.

(Widdowson, 1979: 206–7)

The expected role of the interviewee is disturbed, but more importantly the expected role of the woman is disturbed. What might appear to be a humorous example of inappropriate discourse is also, importantly, a recognition of different cultural expectations for drama texts, and, in my reading, of the injustices meted out to women and the need for that to be made clear. Whether that is necessarily the best strategy for getting the job is another matter, but there comes a time when it becomes politically necessary to shift what is appropriate discourse from one context into what might be considered as an inappropriate context in order to effect change. It is a process of de-stabilisation.

Subjectivity

Contemporary critical practice makes a distinction between a speaking 'individual' and 'subject position'. It does so to avoid the kind of discussion that takes place in more traditional ways of thinking which sees the 'individual', particularly in creative fields, as unique and rather more sensitive than others, a product of their own 'in-built' talents, rather than a product of social, institutional, discursive determinations. A contemporary position would argue that we are *interpellated* as subjects, rather than born with a unique and specific social and cultural identity. We are constructed not just as a single subject, but in many different contexts and situations as many different subjects. Subjectivity is conferred upon us, and we, in turn, confer it upon others. The idea of conferring needs to be stressed here, because what is at stake is an understanding of subjectivity/individuality which is not already there within us. Subjectivity therefore is an interactive process – it requires other participants.

One of the most effective ways of understanding this conferring of subjectivity is to think in terms of *gaze*, and a classic way of understanding gaze is to imagine you are walking in the street, someone calls out, and you turn around. As soon as you turn around you become the object of someone else's gaze. You are then determined as a subject because you are the object of that gaze. The interaction of your being called and your responding is what confers your subjectivity upon you. Different 'calls' involve different subjectivities. Multiply this act of 'turning round' to be the subject of someone else's gaze many times from many different perspectives and points of view, and the concept of subjectivity, like the concept of performance texts we have discussed so far, is one which is best defined in terms of *bricollage*; in terms of multiple fragments rather than single coherent ways of meaning. It is this bricollage of subjectivity which might then be best thought of in terms of *suture*, i.e. the way in which a subject position is put together and sewn to 'reality'. Our identities then, our subjectivity, is socially and culturally interpellated into institutional discourses. We are never individuals separate from institutionally determined discourses. We do not have an intrinsic subjectivity given at birth. We are culturally interpellated as subjects. Subjectivity is not 'natural', it is determined discursively, and that then becomes an important question of language. For example, DUFF and LOCO construct WOMAN as a whore – as 'other' – in several different linguistic ways in *Experimental Death Unit 1*, (Baraka, 1971: 13f):

DUFF: How much are you charging, pilgrim?

WOMAN: I charge just what you owe.

DUFF: Owe?

LOCO: You fool, we owe everything. (*Falls towards* WOMAN *on his knees, with high whimper, finally tears*)

WOMAN: (*screams*) OWE! OWE! (*She grabs at DUFF's balls*) What there is to take. (*Laughs*) From what remains of your dwindling stash.

DUFF: You whore. What're you . . . symbolic nigger from the grave?

LOCO: (*Turning to restrain* DUFF) Shut up . . . shut up . . . This is the time your feebleminded muse, and mother . . . dippy wife, brother should have screamed through the snot of their Wheaties.

DUFF: A whore. A black stinking mess of a bitch.

WOMAN: Eat me, you lousy democrat!

LOCO: (*grabbing the* WOMAN's *legs, as he writhes, though genteely, on the floor*) Help! (*Begins to lick her legs and other flesh*) Help! Help! Help us, you nigger. Help us, slick pussy lady. Let me eat your sanity, gobble your gooky mystiques. Lick you. Let me lick you lick you lick you. I'm an icebox. Heat! Silence! No noise between your hams. Lick and lick. Help, hairy lady. Smelly lady. Blackest of all ladies, help me . . . us! . . . all of us!

DUFF: Get up, you immigrant louse! Spineless! (*Dragging* LOCO *under the armpits away from the* WOMAN) Get away from that greasy . . .

LOCO: I am right, Duff . . . let me go! I know what's needed. I feel it. (*Screams, long long barely human*) Please. I'm right. We die without this heat.

WOMAN: (*Regarding both of them haughtily, taking out marijuana, beginning to pull it up into her mouth, sucking deep*) Whhhh . . . shit, damn queers, Whhhh . . . (*Sucking, fondling the joint*) Whhhh . . . shit. Fools.

DUFF: Shut up or I'll beat your head into some delicacy!

By being called pilgrim, fool, whore, symbolic nigger, a black stinking mess of a bitch, slick pussy lady, hairy lady, smelly lady, nigger, blackest of all ladies, DUFF and LOCO confer upon her an identity of 'other' which defines her by these labels in this particular situation by these particular characters. Similarly WOMAN has constructed DUFF and LOCO as objects of her gaze and conferred an identity upon them as 'other' in her cultural terms, as queers, and LOCO in particular, and relatedly I assume, as a lousy democrat. The actions of LOCO confirm their linguistic labelling of WOMAN, and similarly WOMAN's treatment of them, particularly DUFF, confirms her determination of them as queer:

DUFF: I'm just eager.
WOMAN: For what? Your dick up my butt? (*Looks up, smiling*) Drizzle, drizzle, drizzle, drizzle. Drizzle. Ah drizzle. Go ahead . . . do that right, now! (*At them*) The weather. Your faces. My stories. What are they in terms of the spirit? Aside from droopy personalities that will inhabit the street's longing. We whores. We poets. We wet buttocks in the face of God. We all look, and long and sing.

(Baraka, 1971:13)

But this is not just street language, it is about the multiplicity of meanings and subjectivities. The whore is both whore and poet; DUFF and LOCO are both straight and queer.

The French linguist, Emile Benveniste, has written that 'It is in and through language that man [*sic passim*] constitutes himself as a *subject*, because language alone establishes the concept of 'ego' in reality . . .' (Benveniste, 1971:218) The reality, therefore, to which words like *I* and *you* refer is for Benveniste a reality of discourse. Language is only possible, Benveniste asserts, because speakers are 'set up' as subjects with words like *I* and *you* and with the various markers for person in discourse. We are not, therefore, talking about a 'natural' phenomenon, but the determination of subjectivity discursively. Alan Bold, for example, constructs the audience for his *The State of the Nation* (1969:7) in terms of the following subject positions:

To You: ugly and deformed, stupid with simulated wisdom, resigned to your inhibitions, worthless, wasted;
To you: pathetic, consciously non-athletic, as if immune to looks, rapped in plastic torment;
To you: legislators, arrogant in your ignorant lack of sensitivity, initiating crimes without consultation;
To you: wretched female impersonators, taking love as a slogan for your deep hatred of humanity;
To you: incapacitated morons, smug in your endorsement of apostasy, hating what you were, becoming hateful;
To you: dreamers, exalting your trivial private incidents to universal insights;
To you: drop-outs, dropped out, careless thinkers, viciously gentle, no more than specimens;

And so on until it closes:

To you: who are none of these.
I come with a message on the state of the nation . . .

The *you* is defined by the text, and therefore the performers of that text, thereby putting performers into a much more powerful and more dominant position than the audience/readers. Peter Handke uses this to a striking degree in *Offending the Audience* (1971) and in *Kaspar* (1969) where having learnt a number of model sentences KASPAR speaks along with the prompters who taught him those sentences in a routine that has 27 repetitions of *you* culminating in the prompters reiterating this construction of KASPAR as *you* with:

You know what you are saying.
You say what you are thinking.
You think like you feel. You
feel what it depends on.
You know on what it depends.
You know what you want. You
can if you want to. You can if
you only want to. You can if
you must.

(Handke, 1969:56)

and so on, where the *you* is fronted, i.e. given a prominent thematic position at the front of each clause, and is echoed by KASPAR in the next speech with:

> When I am, I was. When I
> was, I am. When I am, I will
> be. When I will be, I was.
> Although I will be, I am. As
> often as I am, I have been. As
> often as I have been, I was.
> While I was, I have been.
> While I have been, I will be . . .

(Handke, 1969:57)

and so on. The difference, of course, is that the *I* here is not fronted – what is given thematic prominence are adverbials of time and concession – distancing the assurance that KASPAR's identity is secure. But as the speech develops, so does the assurance until the last few lines:

> I am the one I am.
> I am the one I am.
> I am the one I am.

(Handke, 1969:58)

This grasping at individual subjectivity is futile because identity is never defined beyond 'the one'; identity – subjectivity – requires other people, other participants; can only *be* in interaction.

PETER in the television text *Caught on a Train* (Poliakoff 1987:105f) might demonstrate this in the final two scenes when he says goodbye to FRAU MESSNER having spent a considerable amount of time with her, under some difficult and trying circumstances, on a train:

> PETER: I must say goodbye now.
> FRAU MESSNER: Yes, go on then.
> PETER Maybe – (*A nervous smile as she looks at him.*) We'll
> catch the same train again sometime.

He moves slightly towards the door. She turns away, but then looks up as he nears the door.

FRAU MESSNER: (*Her tone is very precise*). You're a nice boy in many ways.

PETER *stops*

You're good looking. You're quite clever. You notice things. And you're not at all cruel. (*She suddenly looks directly at him, then louder.*) But you *don't care*.

The train has stopped.

You pretend to of course, you pretend.

She is staring straight at him.

But you don't really care about anything do you?

She stares at his pale young face, as he stands holding his case.

Except maybe success in your work. Becoming very successful. It's all you have. You don't *feel* anything else. *Nothing. You just cannot feel anything else.*

She looks at him.

Can you?

Silence.

I wonder what will happen to you?

PETER *is staring at the train door, looking bewildered.*

(*Matter of fact.*) You can go now. The train has stopped.

She turns away. She is quite calm, she does not look at him.

Silence.
A noise of train doors banging.

PETER: Frau Messner?

She does not react.
He goes up to her. As he gets up to her she closes her eyes.

Frau Messner?

Silence.
She does not look up. Her eyes are shut. PETER, *staring down at her, moves as if to touch her face.*
Her eyes open.
He immediately moves back.
She closes her eyes again.
He stands for a moment, unsure of what to do.
She is sitting back, her eyes closed, her face expressionless.

Goodbye then. (*He moves towards the door.*) This is my station.

He is by the door. She has closed her eyes again, she does not look at him.

(*Sharp*) Aren't you going to say goodbye?

She does not look at him.

(*Sharper*) Aren't you going to say goodbye then?

Silence.

He half moves.

Do you want to know my name?

Silence.
She is looking out of the window.

(*Louder, more urgent, angry.*) Don't you want to know my name?

31. Exterior. Station. Morning.
Cut to PETER *walking along by blank, white walls. We stay close to his face. He looks shaken, dazed, a little lost for a moment. We stay on him as he passes more white walls and puts his case on a luggage and passenger moving pavement. His case moves away from him, down the pavement. He watches it go for a second and then climbs on the moving pavement, and with his back away from the camera, he slowly recedes along it, out of view.*

Throughout the entire length of their time together FRAU MESSNER refers to PETER only as *you*. His sense of his own identity of himself as a subject (what phenomenologists refer to as *Ich-Vorstellung*), is never reinforced by her. Her refusal to use his name, by framing him only in terms of the pronoun, subjects PETER to being a nameless, unimportant identityless person, who does not need to be remembered in any other terms than a chance encounter on a train. PETER might well be performed, then, as someone who before the journey was considerably surer about who 'he' was than when he leaves the train.

Keir Elam (1980:139) talks about drama as being about '. . . an *I* addressing a *you, here* and *now*', as a way of distinguishing it as a different genre of discourse from third-person narratives. Drama, seen in these terms, is about a present, rather than a past, determination of person, time and place because it occurs as performance (at any level) in the here and now. But the here and now, I would suggest, is not a 'natural' event. It is discursively determined by a number of linguistic signals and markers, just as the concept of person is. Subjectivity, like time and place, is not represented by language, it is determined by language. This determination – traditionally thought of in terms of deictic signalling (deixis) – involving the who, where and when of the action and interaction can account for a large percentage of a text using deictic determiners of personal, possessive and demonstrative pronouns; tense; adverbials of place and time, references to the discourse itself; terms of address and naming strategies; honorifics and social markers, and so on. Terms like *I, mine, my, me, you, yours, he, his, him, she, hers, her, their, it, this, that, then, here, there, now*, are crucially important in establishing role relationships, subjectivities and points of view. Deixis is not simply about linking language and situation by 'anchoring' utterance to context (Levinson, 1983:55), a traditional view within linguistics in interaction. It is a discursive, cultural, and political process, not simply an innocent, disinterested means of establishing spatio-temporal relations, or ensuring that verbs agree with their grammatical subjects. Deictic shifts signal different points of view and these in turn determine and are determined by different ideologies. Deixis is a conflict and struggle between *I* and *you*; *here* and *there; now* and *then; this* and *that*, and that often means oppression by stereotype.

Stereotypes

In *Poppy* (Nicholas, 1982) the nineteenth-century Chinese/British opium wars are explored by means of pantomime. That means, for the most part, that in most, if not all, productions, a great deal of humour will be generated at the cultural expense of others. For example:

TENG: And what time is it?
GIRL: The Hour of the Dog is cringing away with tail between legs, whining piteously.
TENG: Do not admit them till it has.
GIRL: Until the Hour of the Monkey swings from the trees, gibbering and exposing itself.
LIN: A most propitious hour to deal with demons.

(Nichols, 1982:60)

The 'demons' are the British, amongst them, English merchant UPWARD and DODO THE DOWAGER LADY WHITTINGTON. The version of 'pidgin' English they, and the Chinese, speak is like this pantomime notion of Chinese timekeeping, obscenely stereotypical:

UPWARD: Hullo, Number One Boss Man. My Number One Shopman Blitish side. Plenty contentee come-see you. Plentee long time my wishee look-see you. All-same Number Two Mandarins they say 'Tomollo, tomollo'. My say them 'Tomollo him never come.' Savvy?
TENG: Number One Shopman plentee too much hullee. Tomollo come bimeby. Like you look-see now.

(Nichols, 1982–61)

What we are involved in here is the production of stereotyped notions of how other, non-English speaking people talk. But not simply as an example of humorous foreigner-talk, but as striking examples of one culture oppressing another by ridicule. The very popular and successful television series *Fawlty Towers* depended for a great deal of its humour on the characterisation of MANUEL, a Spanish waiter, as inarticulate and, therefore, as incompetent. The first programme of the first series 'A Touch of Class' (19 September 1975, BBC2) opened with linguistic confusion about butter portions between BASIL (co-owner of the hotel with his wife SYBIL) and MANUEL:

SYBIL: (*coming back in*) What's the matter, Basil?
BASIL: Nothing, dear, I'm just dealing with it.
MANUEL: (*to* SYBIL) he speak good . . . how you say . . .?
SYBIL: English!
BASIL: Mantequilla . . . solamente . . . dos . . .
MANUEL: Dos?
SYBIL: (*to* BASIL) Don't look at me. You're the one who's supposed to be able to speak it . . .

(BASIL *angrily grabs the excess butter from the trays*)

BASIL   Two pieces! Two each! Arriba, arriba!

He waves his hands towards the bedrooms and MANUEL *runs off.*

SYBIL: I don't know why you wanted to hire him Basil.
BASIL: (*sitting at typewriter*) Because he's cheap and keen to learn, dear. And in this day and age such . . .
SYBIL: But why did you say you could speak the language?
BASIL: I learnt classical Spanish, not the strange dialect he seems to have picked up.
SYBIL: It'd be quicker to train a monkey.

(Cleese and Booth, 1988:3f)

MANUEL is constructed as inarticulate; unable to speak his own language 'properly', let alone English; cheap, because he's foreign, and in a classic racist way is associated with 'a monkey'. He is all set, as *other*, to be a constant frustration to the white (i.e. not-other) British hotel owners, in much the same way as the stereotypical 'foreign' characters in the long running television series *Mind Your Language* were to their white English teacher MR BROWN.

Foreigner-talk exists in all languages but it is how it is treated that is of crucial importance. Freed (1981:32) cites the following exchange, for example:

FOREIGN SPEAKER: I like White Snow and Shop Men.
NATIVE SPEAKER: White Snow and Shop Men?
FOREIGN SPEAKER: Yes, seven Shop Men.
NATIVE SPEAKER: 'Shop Men'? 'Shop Men'?
FOREIGN SPEAKER: White Snow and Seven Shop Men.
NATIVE SPEAKER: Oh, White Snow, I mean Snow White
and the seven short, and the seven Dwarfs.

This is a very broad transcription of a conversation the two speakers engaged in on television cartoons. The confusion arises mainly from the native speaker interpreting [t] as [p] and [b] as [ɔ:] in 'shop men'; from an understandable confusion about the rarity of post-positional adjectives in English and therefore over-correcting Snow White, and from the foreign speaker finding suitable English words for 'dwarf', a word which is probably not part of the core vocabulary of learners of English. The transcription develops this confusion by writing it out as other recognisable English words. The writing-out process has already started the process of the exploitation of someone else's difficulty, and can expand the language problems of others into institutionalised stereotypes.

Is it possible not to laugh for example at AEROPLANE PARKER '. . . a wet jolly Frenchman with a beret, striped shirt, Maizepaper Boyar out of his mouth, soggy bread under his arm . . .' in *The Pleasure Principle* (Wilson, 1974:69) saying things like:

Bonsoir, les Anglais! Fucken wet eh. Wet fucken. Cor. Cunt. Wet. Ello. Ca marche, Robert? Mon petit voyou, pourquoi tu ne restes pas dans la ville en cette merde de temps?

(*he dances about gaily*)

J'ai dit, Why do – you – stay – 'ere, you mad bugger . . .

And if we do laugh, what is the ideological basis and consequence of that laughter? Who are we oppressing?

Peter Mühläusler (1981:105) asked a number of informants to turn 'I haven't seen the man you're talking about' into foreigner-talk. What they used, for the most part, was a stereotyped knowledge of how foreigners – as a single entity – speak, with a concentration on loss of plural marking, loss of third-person morphemes; ellipsis of copula and so on. The results were as follows:

I no see this man
Me no see man you talk about
No see man (*head shaking*)
Me (*point*) no see (*eyes*) man you (*point*) talk about (*wild gestures*)
No seeum man you say
Man you talk about, I not see
No see man you talk
You talk man. I not seen
Me no look him man you say

The potential for humour is inescapable, but it is at the stereotyped expense of others. CLIVE and PHYLLIS in *Season's Greetings* (Ayckbourn, 1982:45) for example:

PHYLLIS: Are you a homosexual, for instance?
CLIVE: Er – no – no, I'm not.
PHYLLIS: That's a relief. A lot of them are, aren't they? Writers. Homosexuals.
CLIVE: Well. I don't know. There's a proportion that are. But then there's a proportion in most professions. Probably no more than there are, say, train drivers.
PHYLLIS: What?
CLIVE: Train drivers.
PHYLLIS: What are?
CLIVE: Homosexuals.
PHYLLIS: Are they?
CLIVE: No.
PHYLLIS: My God, I never knew that.
CLIVE: No, that's not what I'm saying.

The stereotyped homosexual is safely categorised as a writer, (hairdresser or ballet dancer), and therefore represents little threat to male heterosexual society, but to think of train drivers – i.e. 'ordinary', 'normal', heterosexual men as homosexuals is considerably more threatening because it upsets the stereotypes, both heterosexual and homosexual. And in doing that it upsets the 'safety' of a 'well-ordered' society. But more than that, in this particular exchange it generates humour not at the expense of heterosexuals, i.e. the dominant culture in contemporary society, but at the expense of homosexuals.

Much humour depends on this exploitation of others, for example:

> IRISH AUCTIONEER: What am I bid for this priceless vase? Do I hear £5? Thank you sir . . . Do I hear £4? Thank you sir . . . Do I hear £3.50? Thank you sir . . . Any advance on £3. Going, once, going, twice . . . Thank you sir . . . Gone? Sold to that lady for a pound!
>
> (Davies, 1987:45)

Apart from a woman, rather than one of the men in the joke, being aligned with the stupidity of the auctioneer, an area of oppression I discuss below (p. 131), two things, in the main, might be performed here: a joke can be told about the stupidity of an auctioneer, and this stupidity can, in effect, be 'explained' in terms of ethnicity. What would then be demonstrated in such a performance is the dominance of one group of non-Irish people who believe themselves to be superior both culturally and linguistically to the Irish people. But the joke is not context and culture specific to English/Irish, the 'same' joke could be told by substituting dominance oppression relations for French/Belgian; Dutch/Belgian; Canadian English/Newfoundlanders; Danes/Jutes of Aarhus; American English/Poles-Ukrainians, and so on. This is associated, in the main, with ideas about superiority of language use and skill. Jokes like this tend to be aimed at groups of people who are considered to be less skilled in language than the joke tellers. AUTHOR says in *Laughter* (Barnes, 1978:2), 'Laughter's the ally of tyrants. It softens our hatred. An excuse to change nothing, for nothing needs changing when it's all a joke', but this depends, of course, on the nature of the laughter. Simon Fanshawe (*Stomping on the Cat*, 1983) appropriates the language of heterosexual humour in order to deconstruct the disabling image of homosexuality that is usually the result of that language:

I've just been to New York, and when I went through Immigration they asked me if I was gay. I said, 'No, but I've slept with a lot of guys who are . . .' (Simon, are you gay?' – 'No, not personally, I just do it for a living . . .'). One thing everybody is terrified of in New York at the moment is AIDS, the big killer disease . . . it only kills homosexuals, Haitians, heroin addicts and haeomophiliacs . . . I don't know why, the big 'H' . . . and I don't know why it is neither the British nor the American Governments will recognize AIDS as a disease. Now that's strange, because they both recognise homosexuality as a disease. If they think it's a disease, then if you're gay don't go to work tomorrow – just ring in sick. 'What's wrong?' – 'Still queer' – 'Hope you get better' – 'Hope I don't'. (Wilmut and Rosengard, 1989:131)

These are the questions that the dominant section of society (in this case male heterosexual) normally ask of the dominated (homosexual). Their language is that of people in power. Appropriating that language is an increasingly important political move in order to deconstruct and shift unequal power relations.

BLACK MAN and BLACK WOMAN in *Madheart* (Baraka, 1971:63) use a language which is aimed at overturning the white stereotype of black identity by appropriating the language of white oppression:

BLACK WOMAN: (*Her voice goes up to high long sustained note*) I am black black and am the most beautiful thing on the planet. Touch me if you dare. I am your soul . . .

. . .

BLACK MAN: I used to see her in white discotheque boots and sailor pants. (*Pointing to the crawling women*) This is the nightmare of all our hearts. Our mothers and sisters grovelling to white women, wanting to be white women, dead and hardly breathing on the floor. Look at our women dirtying themselves. (*Runs and grabs wig off* SISTER's *head*) Take off filth. (*He throws it onto the dead woman's body*) Take your animal fur, heathen. (*Laughs*) Heathen. Heathen. I've made a new meaning. Let the audience think about themselves, and about their lives when they leave this happening. This black world of purest possibility. (*Laughs*) All our lives we want to be alive. We scream for life.

BLACK WOMAN: Be alive, black man. Be alive, for me. For me, black man. (*Kisses him*) And love me, Love, Me.

BLACK MAN: Women, assemble around me. I'm gonna sing for you now, in my cool inimitable style. About my life. About my road, and where it's taking me now. Assemble, sweet black ladies, ignorant or true, and let me run down the game of life.

BLACK WOMAN: Get up, you other women, and listen to your man. This is no fattening insurance nigger greying around the temples. This is the soulforce of our day-to-day happening universe. A man.

Fighting the stereotypes by appropriating them is a strategy that has been very effective in a number of discourses. *It Bees Dat Way* (Bullins, 1972:6) turns the tables completely on a white audience. The published text calls for black actors and a small whites-only audience:

OUTLAW: (*To somebody white*)
Hey, what's happenin'? What's goin' down?

(*Whenever one of the* ACTORS *start a conversation with one of the audience* THEY *take it as far as it can possibly go in vocal and physical action.* THEY *follow the situation to its most absurd conclusion: . . . Whichever way the audience goes, the* ACTORS *go counter to it or with it, whatever is most unlikely and threatening, even into physical abuse: scuffling, rape, strong-arming and beating the audience*) . . .
(Bullins, 1972:6)

CORNY: (*To white people*) Your mamma's stond . . . you gray-assed diseased brained crackers.

JACKIE: (*To white man*) I sho like to put mah shoes under your bed, mister.

(*She belches*)

Burp! . . .'scuse me, sugar . . . I got a little gas.

CORNY: Yeah . . . I said it! . . . I said it! . . . What you
gonna do about it?

JACKIE: Never mind him, folks. He ain't nothin' but a no
'count nigger.

POPPY: (*To white people*) Don't make no never mind.

JACKIE: Don't pay no attention, ya hear?

OUTLAW: (*To white girl, trying to feel her*) Wha's your
name, baby?

TRIGGER: (*To white girl's friend, be it man or woman*)
We gonna try and help you, dig?

CORNY: Write your name on this piece of paper. If I'm
lucky I can save you yet.

JACKIE: Don't pay no never mind to dese here niggers!

(Bullins, 1972:10f)

This is an overturning of stereotyped white views of blacks by
a reversal strategy which subjects the white audience to the same
sort of gaze that black people have been subjected to for many
years, on the street and in films, theatre and novels.

Ed Bullins, Amiri Baraka and Douglas Turner Ward were
some of the leading writers in black revolutionary theatre in
America in the 1960s, where white stereotypes of black cultures
were battled with. JUNIE in *Happy Ending* (Ward, 1966:13f)
appropriates the stereotyped discourse of plantation slaves and
transplants it into a contemporary urban American situation:

JUNIE: Acting like imbeciles! Crying your heart out 'cause
Massa and Mistress are go'n' break up housekeeping!!!
Maybe I oughta go beat up the adulterous rat crawling in
between the sheets!!! (*Pacing up and down in angry indig-
nation as they sit stunned*) Here we are – Africa rising to its
place in the sun wit' Prime Ministers and other dignitaries
taking seats around the international conference table – us
here fighting for our rights like never before, changing the
whole image, dumping stereotypes behind us and replacing
'em wit' new images of dignity and dimension – and I come
home and find my own aunts, sisters of my mother, daughters of my grandpa who never took crap off no cracker even
though he did live on a plantation – DROWNING themselves in tears jist 'cause boss man is gonna kick bosslady

out on her nose . . . !!! Maybe *Gone With the Wind* was accrate! maybe we jist can't help "Miss Scarrrrrrrrlet-ing" and "Oh Lawdying" every time mistress white gets a splinter in her pinky. That's what *I'm* talking about.

In *Day of Absence* (Ward, 1966) black actors play with white faces in a reversed minstrel show. A note in the published text reads 'Logically, it might also be performed by whites – at their own risk' (Ward, 1966:36). LUKE and CLEM played by black actors are stereotyped white southerners watching the world go by:

CLEM: Do you . . . er, er – feel anything – funny . . . ?
LUKE: Like what?
CLEM: Like . . . er – something – strange?

There then follows a chaotic scene with a trio of telephone operators enacting chaos and pandemonium with 'the line is busy routines' and then:

CLEM: (*Something slowly dawning on him*) Luke . . . ?
LUKE: Yes, Clem?
CLEM: (*Eyes roving around in puzzlement.*) Luke . . . ?
LUKE: (*Irked*) I said what, Clem!
CLEM: Luke . . . ? Where – where is – the – the – ?
LUKE: THE WHAT?
CLEM: Nigras . . . ?
LUKE: ?????What . . . ?
CLEM: Nigras . . . Where is the Nigras, where is they, Luke . . . ? ALL THE NIGRAS! . . . I don't see no Nigras . . . ?!
LUKE: Whatcha mean. . . . ?
CLEM: (*Agitatedly.*) Luke, there ain't a darky in sight . . . And if you remember, we ain't spied a nappy hair all morning . . . The Nigras, Luke! We ain't laid eyes on nary a coon this whole morning!!!
LUKE: You must be crazy or something, Clem!
CLEM: Think about it, Luke, we been sitting here for an hour or more – try and recollect if you remember seeing jist *one* go by?!!!

LUKE: (*confused*) . . . I don't recall . . . But . . . but there musta been some . . . The heat musta got you, Clem! How in hell could that be so?!!!

CLEM: (*Truimphantly*) Just think, Luke! . . . Look around ya . . . Now, every morning mosta people walkin' 'long this street is colored. They's strolling by going to work, they's waiting for the buses, they's sweeping sidewalks, cleaning stores, starting to shine shoes and wetting mops – right?! . . . Well, look around you, Luke – where is they? (*Luke paces up and down, checking.*) I told you, Luke, they ain't nowheres to be seen.

(Ward, 1966:46f)

These are black actors in white faces, remember, wondering where all the blacks have gone from their small town. Their absence creates chaos for the one day they are 'missing'. The Mayor acts quickly once his initial shock is over:

MAYOR: Immediately mobilize our Citizens Emergency Distress Committee! – order a fleet of sound trucks to patrol streets urging the population to remain calm – situation's not as bad as it looks – everything's under control . . .

(Ward, 1966:53)

but of course the whole point of the exercise is to demonstrate that nothing at all was under control. When they finally 'return':

LUKE: (*Eyes sweeping around in all directions.*) Well . . . There's the others, Clem . . . Back jist like they uesta be . . . Everything's the same as always . . .

CLEM: ??? . . . Is it . . . Luke . . . ! (*Slow fade*)

(Ward, 1966:80)

This, of course, is a theatre of direct action which politically opposes dominant stereotyped images of other people, cultures and ideas by appropriating the dominant language. It is a discourse of threat because it is a discourse which demands changes in cultural power.

6   Cultural Power

Gender

In one programme of the second television series of *The Young Ones* (BBC, 1984) RIK boasts of a particular 'successful' sexual encounter:

NEIL: What, you mean, you like – scored – with a chick?
RIK: Well of course I wouldn't put it in such sexist terms, NEIL – but, er (*modestly*) yes . . .
MIKE: Now wait a minute, RIK, I'm the one who gets the girls around here, there could be a copyright problem.
VIVIAN: But I don't understand. *How?* Was she unconscious?
RIK: What, VIVIAN – do I detect a little spark of jealousy?
VIVIAN: I'm not jealous. I find the idea of spending the night with you completely revolting.
RIK: You know perfectly well what I mean. Just because I was the most raunchy and attractive guy at the party last night.
NEIL: What do you mean, RIK, you passed out after half a glass of cider.
RIK: Did I? Blimey, that was a bit anarchic! Well, it just goes to show you, NEIL – even when I'm unconscious I can pick up the birds . . . I mean forge meaningful relationships with birds . . . er, chicks, tarts . . . *women*, women . . .

(Wilmut and Rosengard, 1989)

This is language which constructs women as the sexual objects of men, and as such, unfortunately, is not unusual discourse. What makes it rather more oppressive than 'normal' is that it is spoken by men who are characterised, by the male writers of the series, as male stereotypes of men who could not be, with perhaps the exception of MIKE, sexually successful with women. Both the men and the women are circumscribed by a male discourse which constructs them in negative, disabling ways.

Victor Raskin in a study of jokes includes the following text:

'Is the doctor at home?', the patient asked in his bronchial whisper.
'No,' the doctor's young and pretty wife whispered in reply, 'come right in.'

Raskin discusses this in terms of a frame shift from the frame of doctor discourse to the frame of lover discourse. What signals that frame shift, for the most part, is not just the unexpected response from the doctor's wife, but the shift in roles, from wife to lover and patient to lover. But there is a marked difference in those role shifts which is signalled by the phrase 'young and pretty': only the woman is marked out in the text; the man is not. She is the object of the male gaze and language 'appropriate' to that gaze is used. It is that language which is oppressive because it signals a patriarchal order which positions women as powerless. Opposition to this domination has been voiced for many years now, but, like many oppressive discourses, it is still a major force to be reckoned with. Germaine Greer on the Dick Garrett television chat show in what she assumed to be a serious discussion said at one point to Dick Garrett:

Why, do you realize that this very moment, as we are talking, you are manufacturing sperms at the rate of 400 million an hour?!

to which Dick Garrett replied:

Is it that obvious?

(Raskin, 1987:21)

The frame shifts from serious-scientific to sexual desire with Garrett signalling (jokingly?), that Greer, as the object of his sexual desire, must have actually caused him to produce those sperms. It is not just the frame shift that is objectionable as a marker of a patriarchal superiority which lessens the threat of an intelligent woman by reducing what she has to say to sexual innuendo, but the implicit assumption that the woman is responsible for the man's sexual functioning and activities. This is the discourse of a male dominance which denies responsibility for oppression of women, and which puts the responsibility for oppression (and rape) of women on women. There are numerous strategies for disabling women in this way.

Robin Lakoff and Deborah Tannen (1984) examine in detail the discourse strategies of JOHAN and MARIANNE in the filmscript *Scenes from a Marriage* (Bergman, 1974). In the following example JOHAN and MARIANNE are being interviewed by MRS. PALM for a womens' magazine. They have been asked to describe themselves:

JOHAN: Yes. It might sound conceited if I described myself as extremely intelligent, successful, youthful, well-balanced and sexy. A man with a world conscience, cultivated, well-read, popular and a good mixer. Let me see what else can I think of . . . friendly. Friendly in a nice way even to people who are worse off. I like sports. I'm a good family man. A good son. I have no debts and I pay my taxes. I respect our government whatever it does, and I love our royal family. I've left the state church. Is that enough or do you want more details? I'm a splendid lover. Aren't I Marianne?

MRS. PALM: *(With a smile)* Perhaps we can return to the question. How about you, Marianne? What do you have to say?

MARIANNE: Hmmm, what can I say . . . I'm married to Johan and I have two daughters.

MRS. PALM: Yes . . .

MARIANNE: That's all I can think of for the moment.

(Bergman, 1974:4)

JOHAN is articulate; a 'model' man who not only has all of the 'right' attributes which define him as 'a man', but who can speak about them fluently and without reserve. MARIANNE, on the other hand, needs no language because she has no identity beyond what her husband has assigned to her: namely as his

wife and as mother to his children. In this exchange she is simply
a languageless adjunct to JOHAN. There are other exchanges:

> MARIANNE: I like people. I like negotiations, prudence,
> compromises.
> JOHAN: You're practicing your election speech, I can hear
> it.
> MARIANNE: You think I'm difficult.
> JOHAN: Only when you preach.
> MARIANNE: I won't say another word.
> JOHAN: Promise not to tell me any more homely truths this
> evening?
> MARIANNE: I promise.
> JOHAN: Promise not to harp on that orgasm athlete?
> MARIANNE: Not another word about him.
> JOHAN: Do you think that *for just a little while* you can
> restrain your horrible sententiousness?
> MARIANNE: It will be difficult, but I'll try.
> JOHAN: Can you possibly, I say *possibly*, ration your
> boundless female strength?
> MARIANNE: I see that I'll have to.
> JOHAN: Come on then. Let's go to bed.
>
> (Bergman, 1974:207–8)

Here JOHAN adopts a dominant role, and MARIANNE gives
into him all the time. He rejects her ability with language, and
therefore her ideas, and subjects her to a series of commands in
order, presumably, to make her less threatening before he whisks
her off to bed. His language is the language of directives, hers
is the language of submissives. While Lakoff and Tannen empha-
sise the irony and sarcasm involved in JOHAN's speeches, it is
important for us to recognise that he demonstrates male dominant discourse extremely well:

> JOHAN: I don't have much self-knowledge and I understand
> very little in spite of having read a lot of books. But some-
> thing tells me that this catastrophe is a chance in a million
> for both you and me.
> MARIANNE: Is it Paula who has put such nonsense into
> your head? Just how naive can you get?

JOHAN: We can do without taunts and sarcastic remarks in this conversation.

MARIANNE: You're right. I'm sorry.

(Bergman, 1974:95)

As soon as MARIANNE threatens JOHAN's dominant position by using sarcasm herself, JOHAN springs to his own defence and MARIANNE gives in to him. He forces her to be submissive by, as Lakoff and Tannen point out, accusing her of threatening the stability of the conversation (Lakoff and Tannen, 1984:338). For example:

JOHAN: I have to fork out a hell of a big maintenance, which incidentally I have to pay taxes on and which is completely ruining me. So I don't see why I should have a lot of idiotic expenses on top of that. There's nothing to that effect in the divorce agreement, at any rate. Or is there?

MARIANNE: It's not the children's fault if we're worse off because you went off with another woman.

JOHAN: I never expected that remark from you.

MARIANNE: No, I'm sorry. It was crude of me.

(Bergman, 1974:149)

It is not just the content of the remark that is a threat here to JOHAN's dominance, but the pragmatics of the challenge too. But MARIANNE submits again, accused of threatening the stability of the discourse, and with that the stability and power of male dominance.

BERGNER, a female character in *The Ride Across Lake Constance* (Handke, 1973), recognises this relationship between language and power.

BERGNER: (*To JANNINGS*) Why don't you answer? (*To JANNINGS*) He doesn't answer.

JANNINGS: (*stammers*) Think before you speak!

Pause

JANNINGS: (*fluently*) Perhaps he felt you didn't expect an answer to your question.

BERGNER: Can't he answer for himself?

JANNINGS: I speak for him.
BERGNER: Are you more powerful than he is?
JANNINGS: Why? I mean, why do you ask?
BERGNER: Because you speak for him.

(Handke, 1973:25)

This relationship of language and power is an important one to be aware of in drama praxis, not simply to isolate and therefore challenge oppressive discourses, but to help determine privileged readings for particular performances. JUNE in *The Pope's Wedding* (Bond, 1977) learns how to establish solidarity with the male characters by learning to speak like them so that later at ALEC's shack JUNE plays a significant role as 'one of the boys', and as a woman prepared, by her language, to play the male 'game' of rape:

LEN: (*Off*) Open up, yoo owd bastard.
RON: (*Off*) Let's 'have a look at yoo.

   A stone strikes the wall

JUNE: (*Off*) Oo's got the matches?
BYO: (*After a silence*) Oo yoo got in there, boy?
JOE: (*Off*) We're comin' down the roof.
JUNE: (*Off*) Oo's been interferin' with little gals?
RON: (*Off*) What about that little gal at Finchin?
BYO: (*Off*) An the boys.
RON: (*Off*) What yoo got a 'ide for?
JUNE: (*Off*) Shut up!
BYO: (*Off*) What?
JUNE: (*Off*) Listen!
RON: (*After a pause. Off*) What?
JUNE: (*Off*) I 'eard 'im.

   Screams. Laughs. The noise of tins being banged.

BYO: (*Off*) Perhaps 'e's poopin'.
RON: (*Off*) Do 'e sit on a po?
JUNE: (*Off*) Got any paper?

   Laughs. Shouts. Stones strike the wall.

RON: (*Off*) Bastard!

BYO: (*Off*) Lousy bastard!
JOE: (*Off*) Rotten bastard!
LEN: (*Off*) Stinkin' bastard!
RON: (*Off*) Bastard bastard!
JUNE: (*Off*) Come yoo 'ere and interfere with me!

Shrieks. Laughs.

JOE: (*Off*) 'E only like 'em young.
JUNE: (*Off*) Cheeky bastard!

Shrieks. Laughs.

JUNE: (*Off*) Stop it! (*She screams*)
BYO: (*Off*) Put your boy scout 'at on an' come an' save 'er.
RON: (*Off*) She's bein' raped.
BYO: (*Off*) Don't shove till yoor 'ead a the queue.
JUNE: (*Off*) Next please.
JOE: (*Off*) I'm on t'a good thing 'ere. I reckon I'll put 'er up in the business.

Laughs. Shouts. A shower of stones strike the wall.
                                        (Bond, 1977:300f)

PENELOPE in *Happy Birthday Wanda June* (Vonnegut, 1971:178) attacks the submissive gendered roles that people are expected to play as wife and mother, and also as husband, father, hero, and son. When HAROLD, her husband, returns from his adventures abroad and expects everyone to maintain the roles he had put into place, PENELOPE says to him:

To you, we're simply pieces in a game – this one labelled 'woman', that one labelled 'son'. There is no piece labelled 'enemy' and you are confused.

Similar political positions are taken up, for example, in the theoretical work of Hélène Cixous and Luce Irigaray, and in the dramatic writing of Caryl Churchill, Pam Gems, Dinah Brook, Micheline Wander, Catherine Webster and Joan Ware, amongst others.

Classification by linguistic labelling in this way is a major form of oppression in a number of different discourses mostly by assuming that one label and its meaning is the only right and correct label and meaning. Caryl Churchill deconstructs this, for both colonialist and gendered oppression, in *Cloud Nine* (1979) with cross-gendered and cross-racial characters

CLIVE
BETTY, his wife, played by a man.
JOSHUA, his black servant, played by a white.
EDWARD, his son, played by a woman.
VICTORIA, his daughter, a dummy.

in ACT I, who switch to 'normal' in ACT II (with the exception of CATHY, LIN's daughter, age 5, played by a man) with speeches like BETTY's who is able to assert her own identity by being responsible for her own body and thoughts outside of her relationship with CLIVE:

I used to think CLIVE was the one who liked sex. But then I found I missed it. I used to touch myself when I was very little, I thought I'd invented something wonderful. I used to do it to go to sleep with or to cheer myself up, and one day it was raining and I was under the kitchen table, and my mother saw me with my hand under my dress rubbing away, and she dragged me out so quickly I hit my head and it bled and I was sick, and nothing was said, and I never did it again till this year. I thought if CLIVE wasn't looking at me there wasn't a person there. And one night in bed in my flat I was so frightened I started touching myself. I thought my hand might go through into space. I touched my face, it was there, my arm, my breast, and my hand went down where I thought it shouldn't, and I thought well there is somebody there. It felt sweet, it was a feeling from very long ago, it was very soft, just barely touching and I felt myself gathering together more and more and I felt angry with CLIVE and angry with my mother and I went on and on defying them, and there was this vast feeling growing in me and all around me and they couldn't stop me and no one could stop me and I was there and coming and coming. Afterwards I thought I'd betrayed CLIVE. My mother would kill me. But I felt triumphant because I was a separate person from them. And I cried because I didn't want to be. But I don't cry about it any more. Sometimes I do it three times in one night and it really is great fun.

(Churchill, 1979:49)

Ownership of the body has been an important focus for feminist resistance to patriarchal oppression as well as issues of gendered language. Women, for example, have tended to be labelled, by men (and by women who have learnt this from men, consciously or not) as Deborah Cameron (1985: 35) points out, as disfluent, unable to finish a sentence, illogical, unassertive, using questions more than statements in order to seek approval, less communicative than men in mixed groups, and co-operative rather than combative in the way they use language. Cameron takes issues with these labels, as well as with some of the assumed markers of the way women are thought to use language differently from men detailed by other women, for example Lakoff (1975). While she is sceptical about there being a distinct womens' language, Cameron, like Jennifer Coates, in *Women, Men and Language*, develops an argument about gendered language which draws together many of the important aspects of the way women have been, and continue to be, oppressed by male-dominated discourse. For example, Coates points out that the normal turn-taking system in conversation is always a battle for the floor; always a struggle for who is to speak next and that women have generally been less likely to fight as hard as a man to gain control of the floor by interrupting and overlapping. Coates makes the point that men rarely interrupt one another, whereas in mixed gender exchanges men infringe womens' rights to speak.

Furthermore, the speakers who fall silent as a result of interruptions are usually women, who are often the less dominant speakers. Similarly, silence is usually considered to be a sign of a malfunction in conversation, and the average silence, Coates argues, is longer in mixed conversations than in single-gender ones. These silences result from interruptions and overlaps but also from delayed minimal responses like 'mm' or 'yes', which are usually interpreted as positive responses. In mixed gender conversations male speakers often delay these minimal responses, and by so doing delay positive feedback, increasing the possibility of negative feedback signalling a lack of interest in or understanding of what the woman has to say. Furthermore, men talking to women often deny them the right to control the topic of conversation by using interruptions and minimal responses because speakers who are male and well-informed tend to dominate. Men are also thought, by some researchers, to use fewer hedges and tag questions than women, thereby presenting themselves as more assertive than women.

Discussions of differences like these, and others, have resulted in a call for a theatre language which counters male oppression in this way. To some extent Caryl Churchill explores this in *Serious Money* (1987) where she develops a language which is aware of the struggle for the floor, interruptions, latching, breaching, floor control, hedges, repairs, adjacency pairs, insertion sequences, turn-taking, false starts and backtracks, by marking the text to signal these conversational strategies and giving a detailed note at the beginning of the published edition as a guide to their use. This is an important move, but one which is still in its infancy in dramatic writing.

Carnival and Masks

Issues of marginality and uncentredness are crucial in drama praxis in a number of ways, not least for reading post-colonialist societies like South Africa, where the oppression of one culture by another is constitutionally determined.

STYLES in *Sizwe Bansi is Dead* (Fugard *et al.*, 1974:7f), for example, plays a number of roles as he tells his story:

STYLES: . . . General Foreman Mr 'Baas' Bradley called me.
'Styles!'
'Yes. Sir.'
'Come translate.'
'Yes, sir!'

(*Styles pulls out a chair. Mr 'Baas' Bradley speaks on one side, Styles translates on the other.*)

'Tell the boys in your language, that this is a very big day in their lives.'

'Gentlemen. This old fool say this is a hell of a big day in our lives.'

The men laughed.

'They are very happy to hear that, sir.'

'Tell the boys that Mr Henry Ford the Second, the owner of this place, is going to visit us. Tell them Mr Ford is the big Baas. He owns the plant and everything in it.'

Gentlemen, old Bradley says this Ford is a big bastard. He owns everything in this building, which means you as well.'

A voice came out of the crowd:

'Is he a bigger fool than Bradley?'

'They're asking, sir, is he bigger than you?'

'Certainly . . . (*blustering*) . . . certainly. He is a very big baas. He's a . . . (*groping for words*) . . . he's a Makulu Baas.'

I loved that one!

'Mr "Baas" Bradley says most certainly Mr Ford is bigger than him. In fact Mr Ford is the grandmother baas of them all . . . that's what he said to me.'

'Styles, tell the boys that when Mr Henry Ford comes into the plant I want them all to look happy. We will slow down the speed of the lines so that they can sing and smile while they are working.'

'Gentlemen, he says that when the door opens and his grand-mother walks in you must see to it that you are wearing a mask of smiles. Hide your true feelings, brothers. You must sing. The joyous songs of the days of old before we had fools like this one next to me to worry about.' (*To Bradley*) 'Yes, sir!'

'Say to them, Styles, that they must try to impress Mr Henry Ford that they are better than those monkeys in his own country, those niggers in Harlem who know nothing but strike, strike.'

Yo! I liked that one too.

'Gentlemen, he says we must remember, when Mr Ford walks in, that we are South African monkeys, not American monkeys. South African monkeys are much better trained . . .'

Before I could even finish, a voice was shouting out of the crowd:

'He's talking shit!' I had to be careful!

(*Servile and full of smiles as he turns back to Bradley*.)

'No, sir! The men say they are much too happy to behave like those American monkeys.'
Right! Line was switched on nice and slow – and we started working.

The dominant cultural force here, represented by BRADLEY as white South Africa, is ridiculed by translation. This is not just innocent ridicule – it stands as one of the most powerful linguistic means STYLES, and the black South Africans he represents, have of demonstrating cultural power. This is not simply innocent, disinterested, humour, it is based on a very old tradition of what Mikhail Bakhtin calls the *carnival* of discourse. Julia Kristeva (1980:65) points out that carnivalesque discourse '. . . breaks the laws of a language censored by grammar and semantics and, at the same time, is a social and political protest.'; what Umberto Eco refers to as a '. . . license to violate the rule' (Eco, 1987:275), and is, therefore, an attempt to subvert established, closed, views and restrictions; for example, W. H. Auden, *Paid on Both Sides: A Charade* (Mendelson, 1977:9–10):

X: Stand back there. Here comes the doctor.

(*Enter Doctor and his boy*)

BOY: Tickle your arse with a feather, sir.
DOCTOR: What's that?
BOY: Particularly nasty weather, sir.
DOCTOR: Yes, it is. Tell me, is my hair tidy? One must always be careful with a new client.
BOY: It's full of lice, sir.
DOCTOR: What's that?
BOY: It's looking nice, sir.

(*For the rest of the scene the boy fools about*)

This is the classic carnival situation – it is not just an innocent music-hall joke, it is about power and status and the undermining of the status of the doctor. It is *interested* discourse; interested in effecting some sort of change.

Eugene O'Neill did not include a great many varieties of American English in his early plays out of an innocent, disinterested, love of language. He was part of an informal political movement which sought actively to change people's awareness of the many varieties of American English that were in current use in order to establish an American identity on stage which stood counter to the dominant view that the English language belonged to Britain. Jean Chothia has analysed in considerable detail the varieties O'Neill used and has categorised them in terms of American low colloquial, American idiomatic and Standard American English, developing what might now be considered a sociolectal cline of language varieties (Chothia, 1979). O'Neill was part of *The American Language Movement* along with people like Walt Whitman, Mark Twain, Robert Lowell, Ernest Hemingway, Dos Passos, Carl Sandburg, amongst many others, who have actively selected specific varieties of language in order to make statements about an American, post-colonial, identity. The character YANK, in *The Hairy Ape* (O'Neill, 1923:76) is talking to a caged gorilla:

> YANK: It's dis way, what I'm drivin' at. Youse can sit and dope dream in de past, green woods, de jungle, and de rest of it. Den yuh belong and dey don't. Den yuh kin laugh at 'em see? Yuh're de champ of de woild. But me – I ain't got no past to tink in, nor notin' dat's comin' on'y what's now – an dat don't belong. Sure, you're de best off. Yuh can't tink, can yuh? Yuh can't talk neider. But I kin make a bluff at talkin' and tinkin' – a'most git away with it – a'most! – an dat's where de joker comes in. (*He laughs*)

It is a political choice to write language like this for a particular character standing as it does in marked contrast to a standard spoken and written American English. Particularly when that choice is not just to signal a particular character as 'low-life', but as a perfectly standard character.

Similarly, J. M. Synge did not just use an Anglo-Irish variety of English innocently. It was a political move made as part of a larger move to establish a national non-Gaelic/non-English Irish identity by establishing a national Irish theatre in English. It was a political move against the sort of linguistic conservatism which kept the varieties of English spoken by a large percentage of the Irish population out of the public arena. The language he wrote, like O'Neill's, does not aim to be a close transcription of actual speech patterns, but a dramatic representation which uses selected, often stereotyped, linguistic features. In terms of the theatre of its day this was a radical, revolutionary, linguistic move, in order to establish a radical national identity which stood counter to the polarities of Gaelic Irish and British English. The character CHRISTY, for example, in *Playboy of the Western World* (Synge, 1932:64):

> CHRISTY: It's little you'll think if my love's a poacher's or an earl's itself, when you feel my two hands stretched around you, and squeezing kisses on your puckered lips, till I'd feel a kind of pity for the Lord God is all ages sitting lonesome in his golden chair.

The fronted objects and complements, the marked use of the copula, a greater emphasis on syntax, rather than stress, to develop information structure would seem to signal an Anglo-Irish variety of English. We are therefore talking about the establishing of a language variety in order to establish a national identity, generally, in the wake of the domination of one culture over another. For example, the exchange about the church organ between SALUBI and SAMSON in *The Road* (Soyinka, 1973:161f):

> SALUBI: Why he day come play dat ting every morning self? Nobody dey inside church.
> SAMSON: Rehearsal stupid. You think people just sit down in front of the organ and play just like that? Ah, when Professor was Professor, he would go up after the service and correct the organist where he went wrong. And even during the singing if he heard a wrong note he would shake his head and look round the church making tch-tch-tch-tch-tch. Every time the organist saw that, he knew he was in serious trouble.
> SALUBI: Why'e no kuku play the ting itself?
> SAMSON: Where were you born that you don't know about Professor?

SALUBI: I only know there was the matter of the church
   funds? Did he go to prison?
SAMSON: You think they just put somebody in prison like
   that? Professor his very self? Of course you don't know your
   history. When Professor entered church, everybody turned
   round and the eyes of the congregation followed him to his
   pew – and he had his own private pew let me tell you, and
   if a stranger went and sat in it, the church warden wasted
   no time driving him out.
SALUBI: Dat one no to church, na high society.
SAMSON: You no sabbe de ting wey man dey call class so
   shurrup your mout. Professor enh, he get class. He get style.
   That suit he wears now, that was the very way he used to
   dress to evening service. I tell you, the whole neighbourhood
   used to come and watch him . . .

Codes shift and mix here in an important demonstration of
varieties of English which would be considered non-standard by
colonial oppressors, but which are increasingly being recognised
as acceptable, standard, varieties of post-colonial world Engl-
ishes, not least in their ability to alienate, by code mixing in
particular, the colonial domination by language.

This is what Soyinka calls 'the language of masks' – the linguistic masks of code-mixing which is an important way of developing
a new post-colonial language through recognisable myths and
rituals. But liberation from dominant cultural powers is not just
about using varieties of language which the colonial force cannot
understand. It is also about using their *own* language in ways
that they might appear to understand. For example, the exchange
between LAKUNLE and SIDI in *The Lion and the Jewel*
(Soyinka, cited in Ferguson, 1968):

LAKUNLE: A savage custom, barbaric, outdated,
   Rejected, denounced, accursed,
   Excommunicated, archaic, degrading,
   Humiliating, unspeakable, redundant,
   Retroprogressive, remarkable, unpalatable.
SIDI: Is the bag empty? Why did you stop?
LAKUNLE: I own only the *Shorter Companion Dictionary*,
   but I have ordered the longer one – you wait!

(Ferguson, 1968:18)

Individual words may seem to be predominant here, but what is more effective is the way those words pile up. They can represent the language of a colonial presence which for generations has oppressed other people – in this case Britain dominating Nigeria. One important and political crucial means of overcoming that colonial oppression, and particularly after a country declares its independence from colonialism, is to appropriate the language of oppression – in this case the words in an English dictionary which signal ways in which people can be marginalised, i.e. constructed as 'outsiders', as 'other', by an institution which considers itself superior – and by that *act* of appropriation to 'deconstruct' the language, and institutions, of colonial/postcolonial oppression. As Salman Rushdie has said, 'The Empire writes back'.

Writing Back

A Dance of the Forests (Soyinka, 1963) was written and produced to celebrate Nigerian independence, and uses a variety of English which is deeply rooted in the modernist language of writers like T. S. Eliot, but which is also tied very closely to Yoruba myth and ritual. The language is not the language of Yoruba ritual, nor is it the language of English ritual; it is syncretic, i.e. it attempts to tie together the two cultures in order to establish a new post-colonial identity for Nigeria. Soyinka was searching for a language '. . . which would serve not only to rejuvenate the arid condition of European theatricality but which would serve to integrate the fragmented and even distorted consciousness of the black people in the midst of a domineering culture.' ESHUORO, for example, in *A Dance of the Forests* (Soyinka, 1963:48f):

> ESHUORO: Demoke, son and son to carvers, who taught you
> How you impale me, abuse me! Scratching my shame
> To the dwellers of hell, where
> The womb-snake shudders and the world is set on fire
> Demoke, did you know? Mine is the tallest tree that grows
> On land. Mine is the head that cows

The Messengers of heaven. Did you not know?
Demoke, did you not know? Only the tree may eat itself
Oro alone is the worm that strips himself
Denudes the forest in a night. Only I
May eat the leaves of the silk-cotton tree
And let men cower and women run to hole.

(Soyinka, 1963:48)

The search for a new language results in a search for the rhythms, ideas and myths and Yoruba ritual, but in an elitist 'literary' variety of English which, as English, is alien to Yoruba culture and the mass of people oppressed by colonial rule. This is a search for a national identity which supports colonial high-culture mythologies.

Soyinka attempts to match the language of Yoruba myth so that 'Language reverts in religious rites to its pristine existence, eschewing the sterile limits of particularisation' (Soyinka, 1988:26). This is Eliot's theory of language which argues that a poem doesn't mean, it should just 'be'; it is, therefore, a classic modernist mythopoeic view of language. E. E. Cummings developed this idea in the blurb on the back cover of the 1927 edition of *him*, for example:

AUTHOR: Well?
PUBLIC: What is *him* about?
AUTHOR: Why ask me? Did I or didn't I make the play?
PUBLIC: But you surely know what you're making –
AUTHOR: Beg pardon, Mr. Public; I surely make what I'm knowing.
PUBLIC: So far as I'm concerned, my very dear sir, nonsense isn't everything in life.
AUTHOR: And so far as you're concerned 'life' is a verb of two voices – active, to do, and passive, to dream. Others believe doing to be only a kind of dreaming. Still others have discovered (in a mirror surrounded with mirrors), something harder than silence but softer than falling; the third voice of 'life' which believes itself and which cannot mean because it is.

Soyinka appropriates this in order to develop a theatre of

liberation in order to effect, not consolidation with colonial culture, but a change '. . . however fragmentary, illusory, however transient, however lacking in concrete, ultimate significances, but nevertheless change' (Soyinka, 1988:45). Soyinka argues against the self-elevation of the writer which he sees as a crime, but the

> . . . larger crime, more insidious than the charge of self-elevation in a writer, is however the crime of the patronizing commitment, a refusal to find a creative mode which would not be coming downwards from a very imaginary, creative ideal, to find a language which expresses the right sources of thought and values, and merges them with symbols of contemporary reality, or fuses them into a universal idiom such as ritual. No one at least will deny that ritual is a language of the masses.
>
> (Soyinka, 1988:59)

In his essay 'Language as Boundary' Soyinka develops this idea of the relationship between ritual and a language of the masses by discussing the post-colonial use of the colonising language; for example:

> The unaccustomed role which such a language is forced to play turns it indeed into a new medium of communication and simultaneously forges a new organic series of moves, social goals, relationships, universal awareness – all of which go into the creating of a new culture. Black people twisted the linguistic blade in the hands of the traditional cultural castrator and carved new concepts into the flesh of white supremacy. The customary linguistic usage was rejected outright and a new, raw, urgent and revolutionary syntax was given to this medium which had become the greatest single repository of racist concepts.
>
> (Soyinka, 1988:139).

What he is talking about is establishing strategic options through language for 'African self-liberation'. Using Jean-Paul Sartre's words Soyinka argues that the use of a colonial language by the once colonised serves to '. . . shatter them, destroy their traditional associations and juxtapose them with violence'

(Soyinka, 1988:143). Cultural power is gained by appropriating and developing the language of oppression and using it to oppose the oppression. The praxis involved is one that brings about change through discursive meanings.

Such discursive meanings are never innocent. They are always about power. Political and critical choices come into play when we determine the identity of ourselves and others by the role we choose to define as the dominant one for a particular situation. Talking about a person as 'the one with blond hair and blue eyes' assigns a quite different role to that person than saying 'the internationally renowned concert pianist', 'the very able French speaker', or 'the appalling cook', even though all may well apply to the 'same' person. How we choose to think of a person, introduce them, and talk about them to others is a political act because we always classify them in one way or another. More often than not those assigned roles often belong to an oppressive discourse/regime which sees certain roles as superior/inferior to others, and it is for this reason, amongst others, that control in interaction – defining the situation – is not an innocent activity. A simple example of this occurred as part of a debate, in June 1989, on English language standards instigated by some comments made by the Prince of Wales on what he perceived to be a lowering of literacy standards in the UK. In an article in the *Observer*, 'English – Whose Standards', (2 July 1989:29) Judith Judd includes an interview with Barry Barker, secretary and chief executive of the Institute of Chartered Secretaries and Administrators, who is reported as saying:

> You have to remember that the sort of people who become typists now would have been domestic servants 30 years ago. Intelligent people do other jobs.

One should expect, presumably, that these 'unintelligent' people who are now secretaries will not achieve a high standard of literacy because they do not have the necessary intelligence. What is at fault, following this sort of thinking through, is not the education system, but the social system which has brought into a particular job market a group of people who would have been better off as domestic servants. Barry Barker has a view of certain roles as superior to others which is linked, worryingly, to a view of certain people being superior to others. This is not an innocent statement about literacy standards, but a political view on social networks.

James McCawley (1982:207) poses the question:

> Suppose one of the characters in a television programme you are watching says 'I have more money than I know what to do with' and you are asked what that person has done, how would you answer it, it may be one of the following:
>
>> he said, 'I have more money than I know what to do with'
>> he said something in a very affected English accent
>> he said that he had more money than he knew what to do with
>> he indicated that he was willing to pay off Oliver's mortgage
>> he offered to pay off Oliver's mortgage
>> he displayed contempt for Oliver
>> he embarrassed Oliver's wife
>> he woke up the baby

The character may well be doing all of these but which ones are more relevant than others? Directors and actors need to make decisions about the strength of the signals they wish to give audiences. There are situations where it may be desirable to be as clear in the privileging of one meaning as possible; at other times it may be useful to create ambiguity. Whatever the purpose in the control of meaning, the dramaturgical process demands that the degree of relevance of a particular interpretation and role be understood, and a major part of determining that relevance is a critical understanding of language and praxis.

Afterword

The position I have developed in this book is one which argues that the study of language has to be a study of meanings which are constructed in interaction. Those meanings do not exist outside of the discourse which creates them, and meaning is never separate from interpretation. Meanings are not absolute realities encoded into texts, and are not, therefore, the sole property of the named authors of those texts. Meanings are not owned by those authors, and texts are not reflections or instances of already existing realities. That being the case, meanings are always uncertain and unstable and because of that there will always be conflict and struggle in interaction in order for one meaning to be given higher status than another – one language user to be given higher status than another. The result of that is the interactive base for understanding how language means is based not on co-operation but upon conflict.

Furthermore, I have argued that there is no reason, outside of the privileged vested interests of certain literary institutions, for prioritising verbal language and literariness as markers of 'good' drama, or for considering the production of a drama text to be a staging of an already existing literary text. There are many systems of making meaning, and an effective critical practice needs to be aware of those systems which are often not traditionally included in the analysis of language and drama. That critical practice needs to avoid the tyranny of one system over another. With respect to the discourse of drama that means avoiding the tyranny of single, stable, meanings; the theory of author-owned meanings and the treating of drama texts in a non-performance based critical practice.

We stand, therefore, in critical practice by the politically, socially, and culturally motivated decisions we have taken for a

151

particular reading of a particular text for a particular time and space. Critical practice is about recognising the multiplicity of meanings and interpretive options; recognising that no one reading is correct, but selecting from this multiplicity a particular reading privileged for critical, i.e. political, reasons. This does not cancel all other readings. As Umberto Eco has made clear, 'No text is read independently of the reader's experience of other texts' (Eco, 1979:21). What is important is not just being able to recognise different readings but the ability to make critical choices about which readings are significant relative to a particular situation in order to effect a particular praxis.

Drama texts change according to different frames and functions, different uses and appropriations, and in these changes create quite different realities, as THE FRIENDS OF PIRANDELLO make clear to THE ADVERSARIES in *Each in His Own Way* (Pirandello, 1959:48f):

> You think that reality is something fixed, something definite, and you feel as though you were being cheated if someone comes along and shows you that it was all an illusion on your part. Idiots! This comedy tells you that everyone must build a foundation for himself [*sic passim*] under his own feet, bit by bit, step by step, if he is to advance. You must kick aside a reality that does not belong to you, for the simple reason that you have not made it for yourselves, but are using it as parasites – yes, gentlemen, as parasites – mourning that old-fashioned sentimentality of yours that we've driven from the stage at last, thank God!

This demands that there always be other options, other readings, other interpretations, other realities. Samuel Beckett has written that *Waiting for Godot* is a play '. . . that is striving all the time to avoid definition' (Reid, 1969:65). And similarly in *Endgame* (Beckett, 1958) the search for the 'ultimate' meaning is continually frustrated, it can never be found. Henning (1988:118) writes of *Endgame*:

> Even the ordinary words that remain, like *telescope, bicycle, ladder, dog*, are never simply denotative. Without the restrictions imposed by explicit metaphoric expression or cultural

allusion, Beckett's usage may become more, rather than less, charged with possible meaning, since it may then carry a wider, though less certain, range of connotations.

What we are therefore talking about is understanding language connotatively and abandoning the privileging, and therefore the 'certainty', of denotative meanings. Henning continues: 'A language devoid of contextual reference would be a language without meanings. And a language without meaning would be no language at all' (Henning, 1988:119). Film director Michelangelo Antonioni (1986:10) refers, in a different context, to the creation of event horizons, i.e. where the recession of the horizon is frozen momentarily. Where we choose to freeze this recession is necessarily going to differ for ideological reasons. The result is the formation of discourses which make sense in different ways to different people because they are not generated as discursive formations from an ontological reality – from 'natural' ways of meaning – but from socially, institutionally, ideologically, determined ways. Those realities, like the other side of the horizon, are always fictional.

There is no simple 'real' presentation of self and others in interaction – only a multiplicity of roles which are performed for us and by us, and perceived for us and by us – in different situations. This therefore creates a multiplicity of meanings – a multiplicity of readings/interpretations. There is never a single role determined for an individual outside of social interaction, outside of communication. It is the recognition of this multiplicity and its integral relationship with language and ideologies which is of crucial concern in the view of language I present here, most particularly in its attempt to avoid the sort of absolute reductionism which usually accompanies attempts at understanding 'real' meaning.

Don't act the words . . . act the situation.

(Sartre, 1976:190)

References and Bibliography

A Drama Texts

ALBEE, EDWARD (1964) *Who's Afraid of Virginia Woolf? A Play* (London: Jonathan Cape).

ARDEN, JOHN and MARGARETTA D'ARCY (1974) *The Island of the Mighty* (London: Eyre Methuen).

ARTAUD, ANTONIN (1964) 'Les Cenci' in *Oeuvres Complètes*, vol. iv, pp. 183–271 (Paris: Gallimard).

AUDEN, W. H. (1977) 'Paid on Both Sides' in *The English Auden: Poems, Essays and Dramatic Writings, 1927–1939*, ed. Edward Mendelson (London: Faber and Faber).

AYCKBOURN, ALAN (1982) *Season's Greetings* (London: Samuel French).

BARAKA, AMIRI (LEROI JONES) (1971) *Four Black Revolutionary Plays* (London: Calder and Boyars).

BARNES, PETER (1978) *Laughter!* (London: Heinemann).

BECKETT, SAMUEL (1958) *Endgame, A Play in One Act Followed by Act Without Words, A Mime for One Player* (London: Faber and Faber).

BECKETT, SAMUEL (1959) *Krapp's Last Tape and Embers* (London: Faber and Faber).

BECKETT, SAMUEL (1961) *Happy Days. A Play in Two Acts* (London: Faber and Faber).

BECKETT, SAMUEL (1972) *Words and Music, Play, Eh Joe* (Paris: Aubier-Flammarion).

BECKETT, SAMUEL (1977) *Ends and Odds, Plays and Sketches* (London: Faber and Faber).

BERGMAN, INGMAR (1974) *Scenes from a Marriage*, trs. Alan Blair (New York: Bantam).

154

BERKOFF, STEVEN (1977) *East, Agamemnon, Fall of the House of Usher* (London: J. Calder)..

BERKOFF, STEVEN (1983) *Decadence and Greek* (London: John Calder).

BERKOFF, STEVEN (1989) *I Am Hamlet* (London: Faber and Faber).

BERKOFF, STEVEN (1989) *Decadence and Other Plays: East/West/Greek* (London: Faber).

BLEASDALE, ALAN (1983) *Boys From the Blackstuff. Five Plays for Television* (London: Granada).

BOLD, ALAN (1969) *The State of the Nation* (London: Chatto and Windus).

BOND, EDWARD (1966) *Saved* (London: Methuen).

BOND, EDWARD (1977) *Plays: One* (London: Eyre Methuen).

BOND, EDWARD (1978) *The Bundle or New Narrow Road to the North* (London: Methuen).

BOND, EDWARD (1980) *The Worlds, with the Activist Papers* (London: Eyre Methuen).

BRECHT, BERTOLT (1965) *The Messingkauf Dialogues*, trs. John Willett (London: Methuen).

BRENTON, HOWARD (1980) *The Romans in Britain* (London: Eyre Methuen).

BULLINS, ED (1972) *Four Dynamite Plays* (New York: William Morrow).

CHURCHILL, CARYL (1978) *Traps* (London: Pluto Press).

CHURCHILL, CARYL (1979) *Cloud Nine* (London: Pluto Press).

CHURCHILL, CARYL (1983) *Softcops and Fen* (London: Methuen).

CHURCHILL, CARYL (1987) *Serious Money* (London: Methuen).

CHURCHILL, CARYL and DAVID LAN (1986) *A Mouthful of Birds* (London: Methuen in association with Joint Stock Theatre Group).

CLEESE, JOHN and CONNIE BOOTH (1988) *The Complete FAWLTY TOWERS* (London: Methuen).

EDEL, LEON (ed.) (1949) *The Complete Plays of Henry James* (London: Rupert Hart-Davis).

ELIOT, T. S. (1974) *The Cocktail Party*, ed. Neville Coghill (London: Faber and Faber).

FERLINGHETTI, LAWRENCE (1964) *Routines* (New York: New Directions Press).

FO, DARIO (1978) *We Can't Pay? We Won't Pay!*, trs. Lino Pertile, adapted by Bill Colvill and Robert Walker (London: Pluto Plays).

FO, DARIO (1987) *Elizabeth: Amost by Chance a Woman*, trs. Gillian Hanna, ed. Stuart Hood (London: Methuen).

FUGARD, ATHOL (1966) *Hello and Goodbye* (Cape Town: A. Balkema).

FUGARD, ATHOL (1974) *Statements* (Cape Town: OUP).

FUGARD, ATHOL (1980) *Boesman and Lena and Other Plays* (Cape Town: OUP).

FUGARD, ATHOL, JOHN KANI and WINSTON NTSHONA (1974) 'Sizwe Bansi is Dead' in Athol Fugard, *Statements* (Cape Town; OUP).

GEMS, PAM (1979) *Piaf* (London: Amber Lane Press).

GENET, JEAN (1966, 2nd ed.) *The Balcony*, trs. Bernard Frechtman (London: Faber and Faber).

GIRAUDOUX, JEAN (1958) *Four Plays*, trs. and adapted Maurice Valency (New York: Hill and Wang).

GODARD, JEAN-LUC (1967) *Made in USA* (London: Lorimer Publishing).

GRIFFITHS, TREVOR (1976) *Comedians* (London: Faber).

HANDKE, PETER (1973) *The Ride Across Lake Constance*, trs. Michael Roloff (London: Eyre Methuen).

HANDKE, PETER (1969) *Kaspar* trs. Michael Roloff (London: Eyre Methuen).

HANDKE, PETER (1971) *Offending the Audience; and Self-Accusation*, trs. Michael Roloff (London: Methuen).

IONESCO, EUGENE (1958) *Plays: Volume One*, trs. Donald Watson, (London: John Calder).

IONESCO, EUGENE (1962) *Rhinoceros, The Chairs, The Lesson*, (Harmondsworth: Penguin).

JELLICOE, ANN (1962) *The Knack* (London: Faber and Faber).

LAN, DAVID (1979) *Painting a Wall* (London: Pluto Press).

MAMET, DAVID (1977) *American Buffalo* (New York: Grove Press).

MCGRATH, JOHN (1977) *Fish in the Sea* (London: Pluto Press).

MILLER, ARTHUR (1950) *Death of a Salesman. Certain Private Conversations in Two Acts and a Requiem* (New York: The Viking Press).

NICHOLS, PETER (1982) *Poppy* (London: Methuen).

O'NEILL, EUGENE (1922) *The Emperor Jones* (London: Jonathan Cape).

O'NEILL, EUGENE (1923) *The Hairy Ape* (London: Jonathan Cape).

O'NEILL, EUGENE (1925) *All God's Chillun Got Wings*, 1973 ed. (London: Jonathan Cape).

O'NEILL, EUGENE (1947) *The Iceman Cometh* (London: Jonathan Cape).

ORTON, JOE (1967) *Crimes of Passion: The Ruffian on the Stair. The Erpingham Camp* (London: Methuen).

PINTER, HAROLD (1960) *The Dumb Waiter* (London: Methuen).

PINTER, HAROLD (1961) *A Slight Ache and Other Plays* (London: Methuen).

PINTER, HAROLD (1969) *Landscape and Silence* (London: Methuen).

PINTER, HAROLD (1971) *Old Times* (London: Methuen).

PINTER, HAROLD (1975) *No Man's Land* (London: Eyre Methuen).

PINTER, HAROLD (1976a) *Plays: One* (London: Eyre Methuen).

PINTER, HAROLD (1977) *Plays: Two* (London: Eyre Methuen).

PINTER, HAROLD (1978) *Betrayal* (London: Eyre Methuen).

PIRANDELLO, LUIGI (1954) *Six Characters in Search of an Author*, trs. Frederick May (London: Heinemann).

PIRANDELLO, LUIGI (1959) *Each in His Own Way and Two Other Plays*, trs. Arthur Livingstone (New York: Dutton).

POLIAKOFF, STEPHEN (1979) *Shout Across the River* (London: Methuen).

POLIAKOFF, STEPHEN (1982) *Favourite Nights and Caught on a Train* (London: Methuen).

SHEPARD, SAM (1974) *The Tooth of Crime and Geography of a Horse Dreamer. Two Plays* (London: Faber and Faber).

SHEPARD, SAM (1975) *Action and The Unseen Hand* (London: Faber and Faber).

SOYINKA, WOLE (1963) *A Dance of the Forests* (London: OUP).

SOYINKA, WOLE (1973) *Collected Plays* (London: OUP).

STOPPARD, TOM (1968) *The Real Inspector Hound* (London: Faber and Faber).

STOPPARD, TOM (1969) *Rosencrantz and Guildenstern are Dead* (London: Faber and Faber).

STOPPARD, TOM (1972) *Jumpers* (London: Faber and Faber).

STOPPARD, TOM (1979) *Dogg's Hamlet, Cahoot's Macbeth* (London: Faber and Faber).

STOREY, DAVID (1970) *Home* (London: Jonathan Cape).

SYNGE, J. M. (1932) *Plays* (London: George Allen and Unwin).

TERSON, PETER (1967) *A Night to Make the Angels Weep* in *New English Dramatists II* (London: Penguin).

VONNEGUT, JR, KURT (1971) *Happy Birthday Wanda June* (New York: Delacorte Press).

WARD, DOUGLAS TURNER (1966) *Happy Ending. Day of Absence* (New York: The Third Press).

WILLIAMS, HEATHCOTE (1972) *AC/DC* (London: Calder and Boyars).

WILMUT, ROGER and PETER ROSENGARD (1989) *Didn't You Kill My Mother in Law? The Story of Alternative Comedy in Britain from the Comedy Store to Saturday Live* (London: Methuen).

WILSON, SNOO (1974) *The Pleasure Principle* (London: Methuen).

B   Theatre and Drama Criticism

AERS, DAVID and GUNTHER KRESS (1982) 'The Politics of Style: Discourses of Law and Authority in *Measure for Measure*', *Style*, 16/1. 22–37.

ANDERSON, MICHAEL (1980) 'Word and Image: Aspects of Mimesis in Contemporary British Theatre', *Themes in Drama*, 2, 139–53.

ANTONIONI, MICHELANGELO (1986) *That Bowling Alley on the Tiber. Tales of a Director*, trs. William Arrowsmith (New York: OUP).

ARDEN, JOHN (1977) *To Present the Pretence. Essays on the Theatre and its Public* (London: Eyre Methuen).

ARMES, ROY (1976) *The Ambiguous Image. Narrative Style in Modern European Cinema* (London: Secker and Warburg).

ARTAUD, ANTONIN (1958) *The Theater and its Double*, trs. M. C. Richards (New York: Grove Press).

BARBERA, J. W. (1981) 'Ethical Perversity in America: Some Observations on David Mamet's *American Buffalo*', *Modern Drama*, 24, 270–5.

BARTHES, ROLAND (1979) 'Barthes on Theatre', trs. P. W. Mathers, *Theatre Quarterly*, 9/33, 25–30.

BASNETT-MCGUIRE, SUSAN (1980) 'An Introduction to Theatre Semiotics', *Theatre Quarterly*, 10/38, 47–54.

BIGSBY, C. W. E. (ed.) (1981a) *Contemporary English Drama*, (London: Edward Arnold).

BIGSBY, C. W. E. (1981b) 'The Language of Crisis in British Theatre: the Drama of Cultural Pathology', in Bigsby (ed.) (1981a), 11–52.

BRADBROOK, MURIEL (1972) *Literature in Action. Studies in Continental and Commonwealth Society* (London: Chatto and Windus).

BROOK, PETER (1986) *The Empty Space* (London: Macgibbon and Kee).

BROOKER, PETER (1988) *Bertolt Brecht. Dialectics, Poetry, Politics* (London: Croom Helm).

BROWN, JOHN RUSSELL (1972) *Theatre Language. A Study of Arden, Osborne, Pinter and Wesker* (London: Allen Lane).

BROWN, ROGER and ALBERT GILMAN (1989) 'Politeness Theory and Shakespeare's Four Major Tragedies', *Language in Society*, 18, 159–212.

BURTON, DEIRDRE (1980) *Dialogue and Discourse. A Sociolinguistic Approach to Modern Drama Dialogue and Naturally Occurring Conversation* (London: Routledge and Kegan Paul).

CAPLAN, JAY (1985) *Framed Narratives* (Manchester: Manchester University Press).

CARROLL, DENNIS (1987) *David Mamet* (London: Macmillan).

CARTELLI, THOMAS (1986) 'Ideology and subversion in the Shakespearian Set Speech', *English Literary History*, 53/1, 1–25.

CASE, SUE-ELLEN (1988) *Feminism and Theatre* (London: Macmillan).

CAVE, RICHARD ALLEN (1987) *New British Drama in Performance on the London Stage: 1970 to 1985* (Gerrard's Cross: Colin Smythe).

CHOTHIA, JEAN (1979) *Forging a Language. A Study of the Plays of Eugene O'Neill* (Cambridge: CUP).

COHN, RUBY (1971) *Dialogue in American Drama* (Bloomington, US: Indiana University Press).

CONNOR, STEVEN (1988) *Samuel Beckett, Repetition, Theory and Text* (Oxford: Blackwell).

COOPER, MARILYN M. (1987) 'Shared Knowledge and *Betrayal*', *Semiotica*, 64/1–2, 99–118.

CURTIS, JERRY L. (1974) The World is a Stage: Sartre Versus Genet', *Modern Drama*, 17, 33–41.

DAWICK, JOHN (1971) ' "Punctuation" and Patterning in *The Homecoming*', *Modern Drama*, 14, 137–46.

DE TORO, FERNANDO (1988) 'Towards a Socio-Semiotics of the Theater', *Semiotica*, 72/1–2, 37–70.

DIDEROT, DENIS (1883) *The Paradox of Acting*, trs. W. H. Pollock, (London: Chatto and Windus).

DONOGHUE, DENIS (1959) *The Third Voice. Modern British and American Verse Drama* (Princeton: Princeton University Press).

EILENBERG, LAWRENCE I. (1975) 'Rehearsal as Critical Method: Pinter's *Old Times*', *Modern Drama*, 18, 385–92.

ELAM, KEIR (1980) *The Semiotics of Theatre and Drama* (London: Methuen).

ELVGREN JR, GILLETTE (1975) 'Peter Terson's Vale of Evesham', *Modern Drama*, 18, 173–87.

EVANS, GARETH LLOYD (1977) *The Language of Modern Drama*, (London: Dent).

EVANS, GARETH LLOYD and BARBARA (eds) (1985) *Plays in Review, 1956–1980, British Drama and the Critics* (London: Batsford).

FERGUSON, JOHN (1968) 'Nigerian Drama in English', *Modern Drama*, 11, 10–26.

FINTER, HELGA (1983) 'Experimental Theatre and Semiology of Theatre: The Theatricalisation of Voice', trs. E. A. Walker and Kathryn Grardal, *Modern Drama*, 26, 501–17.

FISCHER-LICHTE, ERIKA (1984) 'The Dramatic Dialogue – Oral or Literary Communication', in Schmicl and van Kesteren (eds), 1984, 137–73.

FISCHER-LICHTE, ERIKA (1987) 'Performance as an Interpretant of the Drama', *Semiotica* 64/3–4, 197–212.

GAGGI, SILVIO (1981) 'Pinter's *Betrayal*: Problems of Language or Grand Metatheatre?', *Theatre Journal*, 33/4, 504–16.

GANZ, ARTHUR (1967) 'J. M. Synge and the Drama of Art', *Modern Drama*, 10, 57–68.

GAUTAM, KRIPA (1987) 'Pinter's *The Caretaker*. A Study in Conversational Analysis, *Journal of Pragmatics*, 11, 49–59.

GAUTAM, KRIPA and MANJULA SHARMA (1986) 'Dialogue in *Waiting for Godot* and Grice's Concept of Implicature', *Modern Drama*, 29, 580–6.

GIDALL, PETER (1986) *Understanding Beckett. A Study of Monologue and Gestures in the Words of Samuel Beckett* (London: Macmillan).

GREGORY, MICHAEL (1982) 'Hamlet's Voice: Aspects of Text Formation and Cohesion in a Soliloquy', *Forum Linguisticum*, 7/2, 107–22.

GROTOWSKI, JERZY (1969) *Towards a Poor Theatre*, ed. Eugenio Barba (London: Methuen).

HAY, MALCOLM and PHILIP ROBERTS (1980) *Bond. A Study of His Plays* (London: Eyre Methuen).

HAYMAN, RONALD (1977) *Artaud and After* (London: OUP).

HEILMAN, ROBERT and CLEANTH BROOKS (1945) *Understanding Drama* (New York: Henry Holt).

HENNING, SYLVIE DEBEVEC (1988) *Beckett's Criticial Complicity, Carnival, Contestation and Tradition* (Lexington: University Press of Kentucky).

HESS-LUTTICH, ERNST, W. B. (1985) 'Dramatic Discourse', in van Dijk (ed.) (1985), 199–214.

HOBSON, DOROTHY (1982) *'Crossroads'. The Drama of a Soap Opera* (London: Methuen).

HODGE, ROBERT and GUNTHER KRESS (1982) 'The Semiotics of Love and Power. *King Lear* and a New Stylistics', *Southern Review*, 15/2, 143–56.

HOMAN, SIDNEY (1984) *Beckett's Theatres. Interpretations for Performance* (Lewisburg: Bucknell University Press).

HORNBY, RICHARD (1977) *Script into Performance. A Structuralist View of Play Production* (Austin: University of Texas Press).

INGARDEN, ROMAN (1973) *The Literary Work or Art. An Investigation on the Borderlines of Ontology, Logic and the Theory of Literature. With an Appendix on the Functions of Language in the Theater*, trs, G. G. Grabowicz (Evanston: Northwestern University Press).

ISER WOLFGANG (1966) 'Samuel Beckett's Dramatic Language', trs. Ruby Cohn, *Modern Drama*, 9, 251–59.

IZARD, BARBARA and CLARA HIERONYMUS (1970) *'Requiem for a Nun', Onstage and Off* (Nashville: Aurora).

KAVANAGH, ROBERT (1985) *Theatre and Cultural Struggle in South Africa* (London: Zed Books).

KENNEDY, ANDREW (1973) 'The Absurd and the Hyper-Articulate in Shaw's Dramatic Language', *Modern Drama*, 16, 185–92.

KENNEDY, ANDREW (1975) *Six Dramatists in Search of a Language. Studies in Dramatic Language* (Cambridge: CUP).

KIBERD, DECLAN (1979) *Synge and the Irish Language* (London: Macmillan).

LABELLE, MAURICE M. (1972/3) 'Artaud's Use of Language, Sound and Tone', *Modern Drama* 15, 383–90.

LAKOFF, ROBIN and DEBORAH TANNEN (1984) 'Conversational Strategy and Metastrategy in a Pragmatic Theory: the Example of *Scenes From a Marriage*', *Semiotica*, 49/3–4. 323–46.

LAMONT, ROSETTE C. 'From *Macbeth* to *Macbett*', *Modern Drama*, 15, 231–53.

LAUGHLIN, KAREN (1985) 'Beckett's Three Dimensions: Narration, Dialogue and the Role of Reader in *Play*', *Modern Drama*, 28, 329–40.

LIGHTFOOT, MARJORIE J. (1969) 'The Uncommon Cocktail Party', *Modern Drama*, 11, 382–95.

MACKENDRICK, JOHN (1978) 'Some Reflections of a Resident Dramatist', *Theatre Quarterly*, 8/31, 3–6.

MAROWITZ, CHARLES (1978) *The Act of Being* (London: Secker and Warburg).

MARANCA, BONNIE (ed.) (1981) *American Dreams: The Imagination of Sam Shepard* (New York: Performing Arts Journal Publications).

MELROSE, SUSAN F. and ROBIN MELROSE (1988) 'Drama, "Style", Stage' in Birch and O'Toole (eds) (1988) 98–110.

MITCHELL, TONY (1984) *Dario Fo Peoples' Court Jester* (London: Methuen).

MORRISON, KRISTIN (1983) *Canters and Chronicles. The Use of Narrative in the Plays of Samuel Beckett and Harold Pinter* (Chicago: University of Chicago Press).

MOTTRAM, ERIC (1984) 'The Vital Language of Impotence', *Gambit*, 41/11, 47–57.

NICKSON, RICHARD (1984) 'Using Words on the Stage: Shaw and Granville-Barker', *Modern Drama*, 27, 409–19.

PAGE, ROBERT (1978) '*Lavender Blue* and the Critics at the Cottesloe', *Theatre Quarterly*, 8/29, 39–44.

PAVIS, PATRICE (1981) 'Semiology and the Vocabulary of the Theatre', *Theatre Quarterly*, 10/40, 74/8.

PFISTER, MANFRED (1988) *The Theory and Analysis of Drama*, trs. John Holliday (Cambridge: CUP).

PINTER, HAROLD (1976b) 'Writing for the Theatre' in Pinter, 1976a, 9–16.

PRICE, ALAN (1961) *Synge and Anglo-Irish Drama* (London: Methuen).

QUIGLEY, AUSTIN E. (1974) '*The Dwarfs*: A Study in Linguistic Dwarfism', *Modern Drama*, 17, 413–22.

QUIGLEY, AUSTIN E. (1975) *The Pinter Problem* (Princeton: Princeton University Press).

QUIGLEY, AUSTIN E. (1979) 'The Emblematic Structure and Setting of David Storey's Plays', *Modern Drama*, 22, 259–76.

REID, ALEC (1969) *All I Can Manage, More Than I Could: An Approach to the Plays of Samuel Beckett* (Dublin: The Dolmen Press).

SALMON, ERIC (1974) 'Harold Pinter's Ear', *Modern Drama*, 17, 363–75.

SARTRE, JEAN-PAUL (1976) *Sartre on Theater*, ed. Michel Contat and Michel Rybalka, trs. Frank Jellinek (London: Quartet Books).

SCHECHNER, RICHARD (1966) 'There's Lots of Time in *Godot*', *Modern Drama*, 9, 268–76.

SCHECHNER, RICHARD and MADY SCHUMANN (eds) (1976) *Ritual, Play and Performance. Readings in the Social Sciences/Theatre*, (New York: Seabury Press).

SCHECHNER, RICHARD (1981) 'The Writer and the Performance Group Rehearsing *The Tooth of Crime*, in Marranca (ed.) (1981), 162–68.

SCHMICL, HERTA and A. VAN KESTEREN (eds) (1984) *Semiotics of Drama and Theatre. New Perspectives in the Theory of Drama and Theatre* (Amsterdam: John Benjamins).

SHEPARD, SAM (1981) 'Language, Visualisation and the Inner Library', in Marranca (ed.) (1981) 214–20.

SHORT, MICK (1981) 'Discourse Analysis and the Analysis of Drama', *Applied Linguistics*, II/2, 180–202, reprinted in Carter and Simpson (eds) (1989), 138–68.

SIMPSON, PAUL (1989) 'Politeness Phenomena in Ionesco's *The Lesson*', in Carter and Simpson (eds) (1989), 170–93.

SOYINKA, WOLE (1988) *Art, Dialogue and Outrage. Essays on Literature and Culture* (Ibadan: New Horn Press).

STANTON, STEPHEN S. (1971) 'Hasenclever's *Humanity*: an Expressionist Morality Play', *Modern Drama*, 13, 406–17.

STATES, BERT O. (1983) 'The Dog on Stage: Theater as Phenomenon', *New Literary History*, 14/2, 373–88.

STYAN, J. L. (1960) *The Elements of Drama* (Cambridge: CUP).

SZONDI, PETER (1987) *Theory of the Modern Drama*, trs, Michael Hays (Cambridge: Polity Press).

UBERSFELD, ANNE (1977) 'The Pleasure of the Spectator', trs. Pierre Bouillaguet and Charles Jose, *Modern Drama*, 25, 127–39.

WANDER, MICHELINE (1987) *Look Back in Gender. Sexuality and the Family in Post-war British Drama* (London: Methuen).

WEST, E. J. (ed.) (1958) *Shaw on Theatre* (London: Macgibbon and Kee).

WILLETT, JOHN (trs. and ed.) (1964) *Brecht on Theatre*, 2nd. ed. 1974 (London: Methuen).

WILSON, SNOO (1980) 'A Theatre of Light, Space and Time', *Theatre Quarterly*, 10/37, 3–18.

WRAY, PHOEBE (1970/1) 'Pinter's Dialogue: The Play on Words', *Modern Drama*, 13, 418–22.

WRIGHT, ELISABETH (1989) *Postmodern Brecht. A Re-Presentation* (London: Routledge and Kegan Paul).

ZILLIACUS, CLAS (1970) 'Samuel Beckett's *Embers*: "A Matter of Fundamental Sounds" ', *Modern Drama*, 13, 216–25.

C Language, Theory and Criticism

ALLEN, KEITH (1986) *Linguistic Meaning* (New York: Routledge and Kegan Paul).

ASHCROFT, BILL, GARETH GRIFFITHS and HELEN TIFFIN (1989) *The Empire Writes Back. Theory and Practice in Post-Colonial Literature* (London: Routledge).

BACHELARD, GASTON (1964) *The Poetics of Space*, trs. Maria Jolas (Boston: Beacon Press).

BAKHTIN, M. M. (1981) *The Dialogic Imagination*, trs. Caryl Emerson and Michael Holquist (Austin, US: University of Texas Press).

BARTHES, ROLAND (1968) 'The Death of the Author', in Caughie (ed.) (1981), 208–13.

BARTHES, ROLAND (1975) *The Pleasure of the Text* (New York: Hill and Wang).

BARTHES, ROLAND (1977) *Image, Music, Text*, trs. Stephen Heath, (London: Fontana).

BEAUGRANDE, DE, R. and W. DRESSLER (1981) *Introduction to Textlinguistics* (London: Longman).

BENVENISTE, EMILE (1971) *Problems in General Linguistics*, trs. Mary Elizabeth Meek (Florida: University of Miami Press).

BELSEY, CATHERINE (1989) 'Towards Cultural History – in Theory and Practice', *Textual Practice*, 3/2, 159–72.

BERGER, PETER and THOMAS LUCKMANN (1967) *The Social Construction of Reality. A Treatise in the Sociology of Knowledge* (Harmondsworth: Penguin).

BERNSTEIN, RICHARD J. (1972) *Praxis and Action* (London: Duckworth).

BIRCH, DAVID (1989a) *Language, Literature and Critical Practice. Ways of Analysing Text* (London: Routledge).

BIRCH, DAVID (1989b) ' "Working Effects with Words" – Whose Words?: Stylistics and Reader Intertextuality', in R. Carter and P. Simpson (eds) *Language, Discourse and Literature. An Introductory Reader in Discourse Stylistics* (London: Unwin Hyman) pp. 259–77.

BIRCH, DAVID and MICHAEL O'TOOLE (eds) (1988) *Functions of Style* (London: Frances Pinter).

BLAKE, N. F. (1981) *The Use of Non-Standard Language in English Literature* (London: André Deutsch).

BLOOM, H., P. DE MAN, J. DERRIDA, G. HARTMAN and J. HILLIS MILLER (eds) (1979), *Deconstruction and Criticism*, (New York: Continuum).

BOLINGER, DWIGHT (1980) *Language the Loaded Weapon. The Use and Abuse of Language Today* (London: Longman).

BROWN, PENELOPE and STEPHEN C. LEVINSON (1987) *Politeness. Some Universals in Language Usage* (Cambridge: CUP).

CAMERON, DEBORAH (1985) *Feminism and Linguistic Theory* (London: Macmillan).

CARROLL, DAVID (1983) 'The Alterity of Discourse: Form, History and the Question of the Political in M. M. Bakhtin', *Diacritics*, 13/2, 65–83.

CARTER, RONALD and PAUL SIMPSON (1989) *Language, Discourse and Literature. An Introductory Reader in Discourse Stylistics* (London: Unwin Hyman).

CAUGHIE, JOHN (ed.) (1981) *Theories of Authorship. A Reader.* (London: RKP in association with the British Film Institute).

CIXOUS, HÉLÈNE (1981) 'The Laugh of the Medusa', in Marks and de Coutivron (eds) (1981).

COATES, JENNIFER (1986) *Women, Men and Language* (London: Longman).

COWARD, ROSALIND and JOHN ELLIS (1977) *Language and Materialism. Developments in the Semiology and the Theory of the Subject* (London: Routledge and Kegan Paul).

DAVIES, CHRISTINE (1987) 'Language, Identity and Ethnic Jokes About Stupidity', *International Journal of the Sociology of Language*, 65, 39–52.

DELEUZE, GILLES (1962) *Nietzsche and Philosophy*, 1983 ed. trs. Hugh Tomlinson (London: The Athlone Press).

DELEUZE, GILLES (1968) *Difference et Repetition* (Parts: Presses Universitaires de France).

DERRIDA, JACQUES (1978) *Writing and Difference*, trs. Alan Bass (London: Routledge and Kegan Paul).

DERRIDA, JACQUES (1979) 'Living On', in Bloom *et al.* (eds.) (1979), 75–176.

DERRIDA, JACQUES (1982) *Margins of Philosophy*, tr. Alan Bass (Brighton: Harvester Press).

ECO, UMBERTO (1979) *The Role of the Reader. Explorations in the Semantics of Texts* (Bloomington, US: Indiana University Press).

ECO, UMBERTO (1987) *Travels in Hyperreality*, trs. William Weaver (London: Pan).

FAIRCLOUGH, NORMAN (1988) 'Register, Power and Socio-Semantic Change', in Birch and O'Toole (eds) (1988), 111–25.

FAIRCLOUGH, NORMAN (1989) *Language and Power* (London: Longman).

FOUCAULT, MICHEL (1969) 'What is an Author', in Caughie (ed.) (1981).

FOUCALT, MICHEL (1976) *The Birth of the Clinic. An Archaeology of Medical Perception*, trs. A. M. Sheridan (London: Tavistock).

FOWLER, R., R. HODGE, G. KRESS, and T. TREW (1979) *Language and Control* (London: Routledge and Kegan Paul).

FRASER, BRUCE and WILLIAM NOLEN (1981) 'The Association of

Deference with Linguistic Form', *International Journal of the Sociology of Language*, 27, 93–109.

FREED, BARBARA (1981) 'Foreigner Talk, Baby Talk, Native Talk', *International Journal of the Sociology of Language*, 28, pp. 19–40.

FROW, JOHN (1986) *Marxism and Literary History* (Oxford: Blackwell).

GADAMER, HANS-GEORG (1975) *Truth and Method* (London: Sheed and Ward).

GOFFMAN, ERVING (1969) *The Presentation of Self in Everyday Life* (London: Allen Lane Press).

GOFFMAN, ERVING (1974) *Frame Analysis. An Essay on the Organization of Experience* (Cambridge, Mass.: Harvard University Press).

GOFFMAN, ERVING (1976) 'Performances', in Schechner and Schumann (eds) (1976), 89–96.

HALLIDAY, M. A. K. (1978) *Language as Social Semiotic. The Social Interpretation of Meaning* (London: Edward Arnold).

HARRIS, SANDRA (1984) 'Questions as a Mode of Control in Magistrates' Courts', *International Journal of the Sociology of Language*, 49, 5–27.

HARTLEY, JOHN and MARTIN MONTGOMERY (1985) 'Representations and Relations: Ideology and Power in Press and TV News', in van Dijk (ed.) (1985), 233–69.

HODGE, R. and G. KRESS (1988) *Social Semiotics* (Cambridge: Polity Press).

KRESS, G. (1985) *Linguistic Processes in Sociocultural Practice*, (Geelong, Australia: Deakin University Press).

KRESS, G. (ed.) (1988) *Communication and Culture: An Introduction* (Sydney: New South Wales University Press).

KRESS, G. and R. HODGE (1979) *Language as Ideology* (London: Routledge and Kegan Paul).

KRESS, G. and T. THREADGOLD (1988) 'Towards a Social Theory of Genre', *Southern Review*, 21/3, 215–43.

KRISTEVA, JULIA (1980) *Desire in Language. A Semiotic Approach to Literature and Art*, ed. Leon S. Roudiez, trs. Thomas Gora, Alice Jardine and Leon S. Roudiez (Oxford: Basil Blackwell).

LAKOFF, ROBIN (1975) *Language and Women's Place* (New York: Harper).

LEMKE, JAY L. (1989) 'Semantics and Social Values', *Word*, 40/1–2, 37–50.

LEVINSON, STEPHEN (1983) *Pragmatics* (Cambridge: CUP).

LYOTARD, JEAN-FRANCOIS and JEAN-LOUP THEBAUD (1985) *Just Gaming*, trs. Wlad Godzich (Minneapolis: University of Minnesota Press).

MARCUS, JANE (1988) *Art and Anger* (Columbus: Ohio State U. P. for Miami University).

MARKS, ELAINE and ISABELLE DE COUTIVRON (eds) (1981) *New French Feminisms* (New York: Shocken).

MASON, JEFFREY, A. (1982) 'From Speech Acts to Conversation', *Journal of Literary Semantics*, 11/2, 96–103.

MCCAWLEY, JAMES D. (1982) *Everything That Linguists Have Always Wanted to Know About Logic* *But Were Ashamed to Ask* (Chicago: University of Chicago Press).

MCHOUL, A. W. (1987) 'An Initial Investigation of the Usability of Fictional Conversation for Doing Conversational Analysis', *Semiotica*, 67/1–2, 83–104.

MÜHLHÄUSLER, PETER (1981) 'Foreigner Talk: Tok Masta in New Guinea', *International Journal of the Sociology of Language*, 28, 93–113.

NEWMEYER, F. J. (ed.) (1988) *Language: The Socio-Cultural Context, Linguistics: The Cambridge Survey*, vol. IV (Cambridge: CUP).

POYATOS, FERNANDO (1983) *New Perspectives in Non verbal Communication* (London: Pergamon).

RASKIN, VICTOR (1987) 'Linguistic Heuristics of Humour: A Script-Based Semantic Approach', *International Journal of Sociology*, 65, 11–26.

SAID, EDWARD (1978) *Orientalism* (London: Routledge and Kegan Paul).

SARTRE, JEAN-PAUL (1955) *Literary and Philosophical Essays*, trs. Annette Michelson (London: Radius Books/Hutchinson).

SARTRE, JEAN-PAUL (1957) *Being and Nothingness. An Essay on Phenomenological Ontology*, trs. Hazel E. Barnes (London: Methuen).

SARTRE, JEAN-PAUL (1960) *Critique of Dialectical Reason 1, Theory of Practical Ensembles*, 1976 ed., trs. Alan Sheridan-Smith, ed. Jonathan Ree (London: NLB).

SCHIFFRIN, DEBORAH (1988) 'Conversation Analysis' in Newmeyer (ed.) (1988), 251–76.

SILVERMAN, DAVID and BRIAN TORODE (1980) *The Material Word*, (London: Routledge and Kegan Paul).

SILVERMAN, KAJA (1983) *The Subject of Semiotics* (Oxford: OUP).

TANNEN, DEBORAH (1981a) 'Indirectness in Discourse: Ethnicity as Conversational Style', *Discourse Processes*, 4/3, 221–38.

TANNEN, DEBORAH (1981b) 'New York Jewish Conversational Style', *International Journal of the Sociology of Language*, 30, 133–49.

THREADGOLD, TERRY (1988) 'Stories of Race and Gender: An Unbounded Discourse', in Birch and O'Toole (eds) (1988), 169–204.

VAN DIJK, TEUN A. (ed.) (1985) *Discourse and Communication. New Approaches to the Analysis of Mass Media Discourse and Communication* (Berlin: Walter de Gruyter).

WIDDOWSON, H. G. (1979) *Explorations in Applied Linguistics*, (Oxford: OUP).

WILDEN, ANTHONY (1972) *Systems and Structures. Essays in Communication and Exchange* (London: Tavistock).

WILDEN, ANTHONY (1987) *The Rules Are No Game. The Strategy of Communication* (London: Routledge and Kegan Paul).

WITTGENSTEIN, LUDWIG (1977) *Remarks on Colour*, ed. G. E. M. Anscombe, trs. Linda L. McAlister and Margaret Schattle, (Oxford: Basil Blackwell).

ZIMIN, SUSAN (1981) 'Sex and Politeness: Factors in First and Second Language Use', *International Journal of the Sociology of Language*, 27, 35–58.

Index